Socialism: A Very Short Introduction

VERY SHORT INTRODUCTIONS are for anyone wanting a stimulating and accessible way into a new subject. They are written by experts, and have been translated into more than 45 different languages.

The series began in 1995, and now covers a wide variety of topics in every discipline. The VSI library currently contains over 650 volumes—a Very Short Introduction to everything from Psychology and Philosophy of Science to American History and Relativity—and continues to grow in every subject area.

Very Short Introductions available now:

ABOLITIONISM Richard S. Newman
THE ABRAHAMIC RELIGIONS
    Charles L. Cohen
ACCOUNTING Christopher Nobes
ADAM SMITH Christopher J. Berry
ADOLESCENCE Peter K. Smith
ADVERTISING Winston Fletcher
AERIAL WARFARE Frank Ledwidge
AESTHETICS Bence Nanay
AFRICAN AMERICAN RELIGION
    Eddie S. Glaude Jr
AFRICAN HISTORY John Parker and
    Richard Rathbone
AFRICAN POLITICS Ian Taylor
AFRICAN RELIGIONS
    Jacob K. Olupona
AGEING Nancy A. Pachana
AGNOSTICISM Robin Le Poidevin
AGRICULTURE Paul Brassley and
    Richard Soffe
ALBERT CAMUS Oliver Gloag
ALEXANDER THE GREAT
    Hugh Bowden
ALGEBRA Peter M. Higgins
AMERICAN BUSINESS HISTORY
    Walter A. Friedman
AMERICAN CULTURAL HISTORY
    Eric Avila
AMERICAN FOREIGN RELATIONS
    Andrew Preston
AMERICAN HISTORY Paul S. Boyer
AMERICAN IMMIGRATION
    David A. Gerber
AMERICAN LEGAL HISTORY
    G. Edward White

AMERICAN NAVAL HISTORY
    Craig L. Symonds
AMERICAN POLITICAL HISTORY
    Donald Critchlow
AMERICAN POLITICAL PARTIES
    AND ELECTIONS L. Sandy Maisel
AMERICAN POLITICS
    Richard M. Valelly
THE AMERICAN PRESIDENCY
    Charles O. Jones
THE AMERICAN REVOLUTION
    Robert J. Allison
AMERICAN SLAVERY
    Heather Andrea Williams
THE AMERICAN WEST Stephen Aron
AMERICAN WOMEN'S HISTORY
    Susan Ware
ANAESTHESIA Aidan O'Donnell
ANALYTIC PHILOSOPHY
    Michael Beaney
ANARCHISM Colin Ward
ANCIENT ASSYRIA Karen Radner
ANCIENT EGYPT Ian Shaw
ANCIENT EGYPTIAN ART AND
    ARCHITECTURE Christina Riggs
ANCIENT GREECE Paul Cartledge
THE ANCIENT NEAR EAST
    Amanda H. Podany
ANCIENT PHILOSOPHY Julia Annas
ANCIENT WARFARE
    Harry Sidebottom
ANGELS David Albert Jones
ANGLICANISM Mark Chapman
THE ANGLO-SAXON AGE
    John Blair

Available soon:

For more information visit our website

www.oup.com/vsi/

Michael Newman

SOCIALISM

A Very Short Introduction

SECOND EDITION

OXFORD
UNIVERSITY PRESS

UNIVERSITY PRESS

Great Clarendon Street, Oxford, OX2 6DP,
United Kingdom

Oxford University Press is a department of the University of Oxford.
It furthers the University's objective of excellence in research, scholarship,
and education by publishing worldwide. Oxford is a registered trade mark of
Oxford University Press in the UK and in certain other countries

First edition published in 2005
Second edition published in 2020

Impression: 3

Published in the United States of America by Oxford University Press
198 Madison Avenue, New York, NY 10016, United States of America

British Library Cataloguing in Publication Data
Data available

Library of Congress Control Number: 2020938618

ISBN 978-0-19-883642-1

Printed in Great Britain by
Ashford Colour Press Ltd, Gosport, Hampshire

Contents

Acknowledgements

I am grateful to all those at Oxford University Press who have helped with this book, particularly Jenny Nugee, who invited me to write this second edition and has provided support throughout the process, and Luciana O'Flaherty for reading the manuscript and suggesting clarifications and improvements. My thanks also go to two anonymous referees and Mike Geddes for their useful comments. Once again, I owe much to my brother, Jeff, both for his general encouragement and for alerting me to the overwhelming dangers of climate change and the need for effective action.

Over many years numerous people—family, friends, colleagues, and students—have influenced my thinking about socialism, both those who share some of my views, and those who disagree profoundly with them. I want to thank them all.

Although this book insists that socialism remains as relevant as ever, it has not always been easy to write in the current political climate of increasing right-wing extremism, xenophobia, and authoritarianism. As always, Ines has provided incisive criticisms and constructive suggestions. Above all, her irrepressible, but realistic, optimism has been of crucial importance.

List of illustrations

The publisher and the author apologize for any errors or omissions in the above list. If contacted they will be pleased to rectify these at the earliest opportunity.

Socialism

Introduction

In 1867 Karl Marx ended the first volume of his monumental work *Das Kapital* on a triumphant note. A point would be reached, he argued, when the capitalist system would 'burst asunder' and at this stage:

> The knell of capitalist private property sounds. The expropriators are expropriated.

For more than 100 years many socialists believed, and many of their opponents feared, that Marx had been right: capitalism was doomed and would be replaced by socialism. How things have changed! Many now believe that capitalism is triumphant, and that socialism is a historical relic that will probably die out during the course of the current century. I do not share this view, and the final chapter seeks to demonstrate the continuing and contemporary relevance of socialism. But whether or not the reader will agree with this conclusion, I hope that the book will at least provide clarification and discussion as a basis for judgement.

The first, and crucial, question is: what is socialism? Those who attack or defend it often take its meaning as self-evident. Thus the opponents of all forms of socialism have been keen to dismiss the whole idea by equating it with its most repellent manifestations—particularly the Stalinist dictatorship in the Soviet Union from the late 1920s until 1953. Similarly, its proponents have tended to identify socialism with the particular form that they have favoured. Lenin therefore once defined it as 'soviet power plus electrification', while a British politician, Herbert Morrison, argued that socialism was 'what a Labour government does'. Yet socialism has taken far too many forms to be constricted in these ways. In fact, it has been both centralist and local; organized from above and built from below; visionary and pragmatic; revolutionary and reformist; anti-state and statist; internationalist and nationalist; harnessed to political parties and shunning them; an outgrowth of trade unionism and independent of it; a feature of rich industrialized countries and poor peasant-based communities; sexist and feminist; committed to growth and ecological.

This book seeks to avoid the dangers of defining socialism either too narrowly and dogmatically or so broadly that the subject cannot be analysed meaningfully. It therefore takes the following minimal definitions of socialism as guidelines.

In my view, the most fundamental characteristic of socialism is its commitment to the creation of an egalitarian society. Socialists may not have agreed about the extent to which inequality can be eradicated or the means by which change can be effected, but no socialist would defend the current inequalities of wealth and power. In particular, socialists have maintained that, under capitalism, vast privileges and opportunities are derived from the hereditary ownership of capital and wealth at one end of the social scale, while a cycle of deprivation limits opportunities and influence at the other end. To varying extents, all socialists have therefore challenged the property relationships that are fundamental to capitalism, and have aspired to establish a society in which everyone has the possibility to seek fulfilment without facing barriers based on structural inequalities.

A second, and closely related, common feature of socialism has been a belief in the *possibility* of constructing an alternative egalitarian system based on the values of solidarity and cooperation. But this in turn has depended on a third characteristic: a relatively optimistic view of human beings and their ability to cooperate with one another. The extent, both of the optimism and its necessity for the construction of a new society, varies considerably. For those who believe in the possibility of establishing self-governing communities without hierarchy or law, the optimistic conception of 'human nature' is essential. For others who have favoured hierarchical parties and states, such optimism could be more limited. It is also no doubt true that, in the world after Nazism and Stalinism, the optimism of some earlier thinkers has been tempered by harsh realities. Nevertheless, socialists have always rejected views that stress individual self-interest and competition as the *sole* motivating factors of human behaviour. They have regarded this perspective as the *product* of a particular kind of society, rather than as an ineradicable *fact* about human beings.

Finally, most socialists have been convinced that it is possible to make significant changes in the world through conscious human agency. It is true that some interpreters of Marx have stressed economic determinism to such an extent that their belief in the role of people in bringing about change has sometimes been difficult to discern. Nevertheless, in general, passive resignation to the existing situation is alien to socialists. They have shared this view with capitalists and liberals, while opposing them in other respects. For capitalism, liberalism, and socialism are all products of the modern era in their belief that human beings may act as subjects of history, rather than having their fortunes determined by fate, custom, tradition, or religion.

These common characteristics help to distinguish socialism from other doctrines, ideologies, and systems, but it is also very diverse. This is not surprising when its evolution and development are considered. If modern socialism was born in 19th-century Europe, it was subsequently shaped by, and adapted to, a whole range of societies. For example, the emergence of communism as a separate strand of socialism following the Revolution in Russia in 1917 (see Chapter 1) strengthened its appeal in many developing countries still controlled by European empires. However, communism was also to assume different forms as it was tailored to local conditions and merged with movements for national independence. Long before the Chinese communists assumed control of the country in 1949, it was clear that their new leader, Mao Zedong (1893–1976), emphasized the continuing role of the peasantry to a much greater extent than his Soviet counterparts, and by the 1960s there were serious clashes between these two communist superpowers. Meanwhile, other communist regimes that had emerged in North Korea and Vietnam were shaped by specific conditions of civil war, struggles for national liberation, and American intervention. Elsewhere quite different forms of socialism emerged. For example, some of the Jewish settlers in Palestine sought to establish small-scale cooperative communities in the so-called Kibbutz movement long before the establishment of Israel in 1948; subsequently many Arab states, beginning with Egypt in the 1950s, turned to a version of secular socialism, modernizing dictatorship and nationalism fuelled in part by the existence of Israel and Western domination. In post-colonial Africa, particularly in Ghana in 1957 and Tanzania in the 1960s, quite different attempts were made to marry elements of socialism with local traditions. Similarly, in Latin America various experiments have been tried, but have normally been defeated, particularly because of the overwhelming power and presence of the United States. The most enduring exception, to which particular attention will be paid in Chapter 2, is that of Cuba since 1959, but, as shown in Chapter 4, there have been interesting recent attempts to introduce socialism, particularly in Bolivia.

Ideally, a book on this topic would discuss the whole world, but this is clearly not possible in a Very Short Introduction. There are also many important issues—perhaps particularly those concerning ethnicity, nationalism, identity, and global inequality—that cannot be addressed adequately here. Instead, I have attempted to examine some aspects of socialism in more depth than would be possible in a general survey, and have also made use of case studies. I hope that the whole work will stimulate further exploration of the theories and practices of socialism.

Chapter 1
Socialist traditions

Some have traced the origins of socialist doctrine to Plato, others to Christianity, and many, with greater plausibility, to radical movements in the English Civil War in the 17th century. However, modern socialism, with its evolving and continuous set of ideas and movements, emerged in early 19th-century Europe. The reasons for this have long been debated, but it is widely agreed that very rapid economic and social changes, associated with urbanization and industrialization, were of particular importance. These not only undermined the rural economy, but also led to a breakdown of the norms and values that had underpinned the traditional order. Liberals of the era welcomed this transformation, regarding capitalist enterprise and the new individualism as the embodiment of progress and freedom. However, socialists dissented from two aspects of the liberals' outlook.

First, rather than individualism, they tended to emphasize community, cooperation, and association—qualities that they believed to be jeopardized by contemporary developments. And, second, rather than celebrating the proclaimed progress arising from capitalist enterprise, they were preoccupied by the massive inequality that it was causing, as former peasants and artisans were herded into overcrowded towns and forced to work in new factories for pitifully low wages. It was in this context that the term 'socialist' was first used in the *London Co-operative*

Magazine in 1827, which suggested that the great issue was whether it was more beneficial that capital should be owned individually or held in common. Those who believed the latter were 'the Communionists and Socialists'. This chapter will examine some of the distinct traditions that then emerged.

The utopians

Karl Marx and Friedrich Engels subsequently attached the label 'utopian' to some of the early socialists. This was intended to convey negative attitudes towards them, suggesting naivety and a failure to root their ideas in rigorous social, economic, and political analysis. More generally, the notion of 'utopianism' has often been used to dismiss projects regarded as unrealistic or fanciful. However, in my view, utopianism is an essential element in any project for social transformation, including socialism, and today's utopia often becomes tomorrow's reality.

The most obvious common feature in the utopian socialists' transformative projects was the belief that a society based on harmony, association, and cooperation could be established through communal living and working. Such communities were set up in both Europe and America, and although they had mixed success, the most important contribution of the utopians as a whole was their delineation of projects for a new society that were actually put into practice. The utopians' ideas and the communities that attempted to carry them out foreshadowed later forms of socialism. However, those who were the most influential at the time did not necessarily produce the most enduring ideas. In terms of contemporary support, Étienne Cabet was probably the most popular, but his notion of utopia now appears dreary.

Cabet (1788–1856) was born in Dijon and, after working as a lawyer, he became a campaigner for workers' rights. In 1834 he was prosecuted for writing an anti-monarchist article and was exiled to England for five years. While there he read Thomas

More's *Utopia* (1516) and this inspired him to write his own utopian novel, *Voyage to Icaria* (1870). All Icarians were to form 'a society founded on the basis of the most perfect equality' with all aspects of life, including clothing, demonstrating these principles. While the degree of regulation and uniformity might now seem repellent, Cabet's Icaria was also highly democratic in terms of the popular participation it envisaged and, at a time when French workers were suffering from extremes of destitution, it appeared to offer hope for a far better future. Inspired by the novel, Icarian societies were established all over France and, with between 100,000 and 200,000 adherents, these were also the most working class of all the utopian socialist movements, attracting fairly low-status artisans, fearful of their position with the development of modern factories. A group of Icarians also sailed to America in 1848, with one community remaining until the end of the 19th century. However, while Cabet had considerable contemporary influence, the key utopians with a longer-term impact were Henri de Saint-Simon, Charles Fourier, and Robert Owen.

Henri de Saint-Simon (1760–1825) was a French aristocrat who defied the conventions of his social class as a student. Imprisoned at Saint-Lazare for refusing to take communion at the age of 13, he escaped, joined the army, and fought against the British in the American War of Independence. Influenced by the relative absence of social privilege in America, he renounced his title at the beginning of the French Revolution and became convinced that science was the key to progress. His hope, expressed in his *Letters from an Inhabitant of Geneva* (1802–3), was that it would be possible to develop a society based on objective principles. His critique of existing society focused on the continuing semi-feudal power relationships in French society rather than on capitalism itself, but his belief in classes as the primary categories of analysis, and his emphasis on the possibility of providing a scientific understanding of historical development, had clear relevance for Marxist theory. However, unlike Marx, he did not see ownership as the most important issue. In his view, history was based on the rise and fall of different productive and unproductive classes in the various eras.

In his own time, he grouped together the overwhelming majority of society as 'productive', while the minority of 'idlers' (including the nobility and the clergy) were 'unproductive'. Advances now depended upon those who 'marched under the banner of the progress of the human mind', above all in industry and science, becoming aware of their mission so that they could effect a transition to the new era. However, this was not simply a replacement of one class by another, as Saint-Simon argued that the industrialists and scientists had a wholly different set of relationships with one another from those between members of the feudal classes. The latter based their position on power, while the industrial/scientific class emphasized cooperation and peaceful competition. The fact that the feudal class still maintained its position was thus a barrier to economic progress and new forms of government.

During his lifetime, Saint-Simon's ideas tended to appeal more to some sectors of the middle classes, who were attracted by the modernizing aspects of the theory, than to the working classes, who were perhaps discouraged by his secular tone in a religious age. He remedied this to an extent in his later work, when he proposed a 'religion of Newton', in recognition of his role as the founder of modern science. Scientists and artists should head a new church that combined a secular morality with a regenerated form of Christianity. The main goals were to eradicate poverty and to ensure that all benefited from education and employment. This widened the appeal of his ideas, and immediately after his death Saint-Simonian communities were established in France and elsewhere. Made illegal in France in 1830, they nevertheless continued to have influence up to 1848, with approximately 40,000 adherents. The Saint-Simonian emphasis on industrialism and administrative efficiency as the key to progress and social justice influenced thinking in many other countries, including that of radicals in Russia.

Charles Fourier (1772–1837) also saw himself as a realist, who believed that he had discovered fundamental laws for the creation of a new society. Born in Besançon, the son of a cloth merchant, he lived humbly in boarding houses and probably never had a sexual relationship. But the utopia that he envisaged, which he called Harmony, was focused on feelings, passions, and sexuality, and perhaps had more points of contact with the movements of the 1960s than with the emerging working class of his own era.

Believing that most problems arose from the mismatch between people's passions and the way in which society functioned, he thought it possible to resolve this conflict through the establishment of so-called phalanxes, or communes. On the basis of a calculation of the number of personality types he believed to exist, he concluded that just over 1,600 people would be the optimum size of each phalanx, for this would enable all passions to be satisfied and all necessary work to be carried out.

Fourier did not believe that people needed to change: the problem was the stifling impact of current society, which was the primary cause of human misery. He also condemned the oppression of women, believing this to reveal the malfunctioning of the social system. He did not emphasize social and economic inequality as a fundamental cause of conflict, assuming that this could be overcome if everybody had a basic minimum, an approach he thought compatible with private property. His comparative lack of interest in the issues of class and inequality meant that Fourierism was the least popular movement of the early socialists, and there were few factory workers amongst his followers. But his belief that human unhappiness was caused by psychological and sexual problems and that the remedy lay in changes in society, rather than by treating the individual, certainly anticipated many later forms of socialism.

Like Fourier, Robert Owen (1771–1858) also believed that society, rather than the individual, was responsible for human misery and social ills. But unlike him, Owen believed that people could and should change. The son of a saddler and ironmonger in Wales, he soon revealed an exceptional flair for business, achieving great success in the cotton industry. In 1799 he bought some mills in New Lanark in Scotland, where he put his ideas into practice.

If Saint-Simon's critique of existing society was based on a kind of class analysis, and Fourier's on its stifling of passions, Owen's grew from a condemnation of irrationalism. His enduring belief was in a form of environmental determinism that meant that people were not responsible for their own characters, which were moulded by the circumstances in which they lived. In his view, the dominant influences in current society were those of religious dogma and unrestricted free market capitalism. He thought that people would act in superstitious and selfish ways because the whole environment promoted such behaviour.

In a *New View of Society* (1813–16) he claimed that, when he arrived at New Lanark, the population:

> possessed almost all the vices, and very few of the virtues, of a social community. Theft and the receipt of the stolen goods was their trade; idleness and drunkenness their habit; falsehood and deception their garb; . . . they united only in a zealous systematic opposition to their employers.

His innovations included new approaches to the upbringing of children, crime, the design and location of buildings and leisure facilities, the relationships between the sexes, and the way in which work was organized. He claimed that such changes, based on the principles of rationality and cooperation, would lead to a transformation in behaviour.

After 16 years, a complete change had indeed been brought about in the general character of the village (of approximately 2,000 inhabitants) around the mills and he was confident that his principles could be extended to a much wider community, for:

> by adopting the proper means, man may by degrees be trained to live in any part of the world without poverty, without crime, and without punishment; for all these are the effects of error in the various systems of training and governing error proceeding from very gross ignorance of human nature.

Viewed in one way, at this stage Owen was an enlightened business entrepreneur, who wanted to increase his own profits by generating more productivity from his workforce. Certainly, his approach was deeply paternalist, and even patronizing, as he talked of inducing good behaviour amongst the 'lower orders'. But although he sought to convince other employers, the church, and the government of the benefits of adopting his principles, their response was one of deep hostility. They feared that the notion of the perfectibility of human beings would undermine the Christian belief in original sin, and his emphasis on the social responsibility of employers to their workers was quite out of keeping with the capitalism of the era.

After failing to win support, his ideas became more radical and he attacked the system of private property and profit. In their place he advocated the establishment of new cooperative communities of between 500 and 1,500 people that would combine industrial and agricultural production. He also believed that it would be possible to abolish money and replace it with 'labour notes', which would represent the time spent in work and would be exchangeable for goods. By now he was seeking to extend his ideas far beyond Britain, undertaking a continental tour in 1818 and travelling to America, where he established the first of several communities in New Harmony, Indiana, in 1825.

Meanwhile, the London Co-operative Society was also established during the 1820s to promote his thinking and 'Exchanges' were set up throughout Britain in which a system of barter took place. Although these did not meet with great success, by the time he returned to Britain from America in 1829, he had gained a significant level of working-class support, particularly when he joined the movement for trade unionism. However, his influence declined after he broke away from this movement in 1834 and failed to support working-class political demands.

His condemnation of the institutions, economic system, and values of contemporary Britain remained wide-ranging, for he continued to argue that these promoted destructive individual self-interest rather than rational cooperation. But he believed that the primary cause was ignorance, rather than malevolence or class interest, and he was often as critical of the workers as the elites. This weakened his appeal, for many believed that pressure and conflict would be the only way to bring about change. However, Owen's emphasis on the importance of nurture rather than nature has subsequently been of very considerable influence on a wide range of socialist thought.

Saint-Simon, Owen, and Fourier each presented only a partial critique of existing society, and the same might be said of other early socialists. Yet taken together, Saint-Simon's analysis of historical evolution through the category of class, Owen's emphasis on environmental determinism, and Fourier's recognition of the significance of forms of social repression provided important elements in later socialist analyses. The utopian socialists were also conscious of the interconnections between the various dimensions of the problems in existing society. This meant that they did not seek amelioration through partial measures: there needed to be a transformation rather than piecemeal social reform.

Though few of the utopian socialist communities survived beyond the middle of the century, they were of enormous importance in formulating and promoting ideas for a cooperative future society in which ordinary people would play a major role. The utopians made a considerable contribution to socialism by focusing on the values of cooperation, association, and harmony in a context of egalitarianism. In the case of Owen and Fourier, this included an emphasis on sexual equality, and there are also some similarities between the utopians' creation of small-scale communities and later ecological thought. They were precursors of an alternative tradition that would reappear in such communities as the Kibbutz in Palestine/Israel, the communes of the 1960s and 1970s, and in the green movement.

Anarchism

Anarchism covers a very wide spectrum of opinion, and not all anarchists are socialist in any sense. Here, I will focus on a distinctive form of anarchism associated above all with Pierre-Joseph Proudhon (1809–65) and Mikhail Bakunin (1814–76). Apart from reinforcing the utopian vision of decentralized communities, its main contributions to socialism were in its intransigent opposition to the state, and its belief that a revolutionary movement should prefigure the society it wished to create.

Like Fourier, Proudhon was born in Besançon in eastern France and his outlook was essentially rural. However, his fundamental values were in total contrast to those of Fourier: he was anti-feminist, homophobic, and extremely puritanical. His ideal society remained one in which independent, self-supporting peasants would study and live in rather basic conditions. But in social and political terms he was far more radical than most of the utopian socialists. His phrase, 'What is Property? Property is Theft', which first appeared in his book, *What is Property?* (1840), was one of the best-known revolutionary slogans of the 19th century. Here he wrote about government:

> Free association, liberty, limited to maintaining equality in the means of production and equivalence in exchange, is the only possible form of society, the only just and the only true one. Politics is the science of freedom; the government of man by man, under whatever name it is disguised, is oppression: the high perfection of society consists in the union of order and anarchy.

His later works were more complex, but there was continuity in his belief that labour should be the basis for social organization and in his opposition to all systems of government. As he explained in *The Philosophy of Poverty* (1846), if people worked just for themselves and their families, there would be no exploitation because nothing would be produced for employers, who had no real function. The first step for the restoration of healthy economic relations between people was to abolish the whole existing structure of credit and exchange. This would also restore the dignity of labour, currently undermined by machines and exploitation arising from the capitalist system. Proudhon also believed that centralized states were inextricably connected with the economic system, for governments worked hand in hand with the capitalists against ordinary people.

Towards the end of his life, he devoted his efforts to considering some type of federal system linking the communities. Such ideas represented an attempt to bypass the state by establishing new structures that could carry out all the necessary social functions, thereby rendering the state itself unnecessary. By then his anarchism had become a real political force amongst a large section of the working class in France, when the doctrine also entered into the mainstream of European socialism and radicalism. However, it was Bakunin who really challenged Marxism for ascendancy in the developing working-class movements.

Bakunin was born about 150 miles from Moscow into a conservative noble family, but was a constant rebel. He met Proudhon, Marx, and other radical intellectuals in Paris in 1840, and read and discussed current socialist and revolutionary works. However, probably always more interested in action than thought, he became involved in the 1848 revolutions in Europe, securing an international reputation as a result. Bakunin sometimes advocated terror for its own sake and certainly shares some responsibility for anarchism's later association with violence, but his ideas were also important. By now, Marx and Engels had published *The Communist Manifesto* (1848) and were endeavouring to influence the European working classes. Bakunin's conflicts with the Marxists in the 1860s and early 1870s highlighted some of the key features in his thinking.

The next section will explore the contribution of Marx and Engels, but Bakunin's major disagreements with them can be elucidated here. The first concerned their overwhelming emphasis upon the industrial working class in the most advanced capitalist societies as the revolutionary class. In contrast, Bakunin believed that the most oppressed were potentially the most revolutionary and that a transformation was most likely in countries that were the least developed economically. In his view, Russian peasants were therefore in a strong position, and he argued that their traditional forms of organization in village communal structures could provide a basis for socialism. Similarly, having spent three years in Italy from 1864 to 1867, he identified great revolutionary potential there because the workers were less privileged and 'bourgeois' than elsewhere. Such people, 'worn out by . . . daily labour . . . ignorant and wretched', remained 'socialist without knowing it' and were 'really more socialist than all bourgeois and scientific socialists put together'.

Bakunin's other major conflict with Marxism focused on issues of organization, both before and after the revolution. In 1864 Marx

drew up the founding statement for the first socialist international—
the International Working Men's Association (see Figure 1).

Bakunin joined the International, but then formed a subgroup
within it to try to inspire its members with revolutionary fervour.
He opposed Marx's idea of creating a (communist) party to win
support for socialism, and in 1868 he declared that he hated
communism:

> because it is the negation of liberty and because I can conceive
> nothing human without liberty. I am not a communist because
> communism concentrates all the powers of society into the state;
> because it necessarily ends in the centralisation of property in the
> hands of the state, while I want the abolition of the state . . . which,
> on the pretext of making men moral and civilised, has up to now
> enslaved, oppressed, exploited and depraved them.

Bakunin wanted loosely organized secret societies rather than
mass political parties.

The culmination of the conflict between Bakunin and Marx took
place in the aftermath of the brutal crushing of the Paris
Commune in 1871, in which workers had taken direct control of
affairs in the city, combining legislative and executive power and
passing a series of radical measures (see Figure 2).

Bakunin had taken this as an expression of his own ideas, viewing
it as the beginning of a communalist movement that could spread
over France as a form of the federalism envisaged by Proudhon.
Marx was also deeply influenced and impressed by the Commune.
But after its suppression, he believed that it was time to turn the
International into a more organized working-class political party.
This move was aimed directly at Bakunin, whose influence
remained strong, particularly in Spain, Italy, and Switzerland, and
Marxism soon defeated anarchism as the major influence over
European socialist movements.

1. Marx addresses the Inaugural Meeting of the International Working Men's Association.

2. Women proclaim 'The Commune or Death!' as they lead a march towards a battle at Montmartre during the Paris Commune of 1871.

Anarchism would remain important in certain areas—above all, in Spain, until both General Franco and the Communists crushed it in the Civil War between 1936 and 1939 (see Figure 3).

There and elsewhere it would also coalesce with forms of trade unionism, often known as syndicalist and anarcho-syndicalist movements, which believed that power could and should be achieved by the workers themselves, rather than through political parties and the state. Like utopian socialism, anarchism also influenced some forms of decentralization and community-based movements from the 1960s. Less positively, since the latter part of the 19th century, some forms of anarchism have also been associated with futile and counter-productive violent acts against individuals.

However, the anarchist critique of hierarchical organization remains important. Thus when Marx was attempting to eliminate

3. Anarchists run a collectivized transport system in Barcelona in 1936.

anarchist influence from the International, some of Bakunin's followers in Switzerland asked:

> How can you expect an egalitarian and free society to emerge from an authoritarian organisation? It is impossible. The International, embryo of future human society, must be from this moment the faithful image of our principles of liberty and federation, and reject from its midst any principle leading to authority and dictatorship.

It was a vast exaggeration to suggest that Marx sought to create a dictatorship over the International, or was in a position to do so. But this anarchist *cri de coeur* would certainly have great relevance in relation to the parties and states created by some of those inspired by Marx in the 20th century. And, more generally, anarchism provides a perpetual warning for all movements: beware the trappings of power and bureaucracy, and ensure that authority is always distrusted. Apart from its vision of decentralized self-governing organizations, this was its essential contribution to socialism.

Marxism

The collaboration of Marx (1818–83) and Engels (1820–95) produced the most significant theory in the history of socialism (Box 1). However, their work has always been open to a variety of interpretations, and dogmatic readings have had greater political resonance than more subtle ones. Since the aim here is to explain the role of Marxism in relation to the evolution of socialist *traditions*, this section concentrates on its most influential contribution rather than attempting to explore the theory as a whole. In this respect, it is necessary to focus on its critique of capitalism, and its explanation of why this system would eventually be replaced by socialism.

Box 1 The partnership between Marx and Engels

The partnership between Marx and Engels was one of the most productive in history, but the differences between the two men were remarkable. Marx was the descendant of a line of rabbis on both sides of the family, and his father had only converted to Christianity to maintain his job as a lawyer. Engels was the eldest son of a successful German industrialist who was a fundamentalist Protestant. Marx showed exceptional academic promise and was denied a university career only because of his political views. Engels was forced to join the family firm by his father and was largely self-educated. Marx was untidy, careless about his own appearance, and had almost illegible handwriting. Engels was neat, well organized, smartly dressed, and wrote very clearly. Marx married Jenny von Wesphalen, the daughter of a baron. Engels remained single for most of his life, only marrying Lizzie Burns, a poorly educated working-class woman, on her deathbed in 1878.

Yet from 1844 the two men were political and intellectual collaborators and close friends. Engels has subsequently been overshadowed by Marx; in fact, he said himself that he had always played second fiddle and had 'been happy to have had such a wonderful first violin as Marx'. Certainly, it was an unequal relationship in some respects, with Engels running his family's factory in Manchester in order to support Marx financially while he studied and wrote. Marx was also the more original thinker, but Engels made an indispensable intellectual and political contribution to the partnership.

The critique of capitalism was embedded in a historical theory (historical materialism). This attempted to explain the whole development of human society. One of Marx and Engels's major criticisms of both the utopian socialists and the anarchists was that they did not deal adequately with the ways in which the present was rooted in the past. Only if these were understood, they believed, was it possible to understand the dynamic processes that would lead to the overthrow of the capitalist system.

Marx and Engels produced an enormous body of work, which has been vastly influential both within socialism and outside it. Yet, despite, and partly because of, the vast attention to the writings, there are continuing controversies over the meaning and significance of many parts of the works. The very short Preface of *A Critique of Political Economy* (1859) was a succinct statement of Marx's theory of historical materialism. In this passage, he outlined the whole relationship between the economic system in each of the major stages of human development and the kind of society corresponding to it.

The way *the material productive forces* (labour, raw materials, and machines) related to each other constituted a *mode of production*. Each mode of production conditioned the 'social, political, and intellectual life process in general' and was 'the real foundation', for the 'legal and political superstructure' and for 'definite forms of social consciousness'. This suggested that the economic structure of each kind of society was the foundation (sometimes known as 'the base') for all the major institutions, including people's social consciousness (world outlook). Thus the nature of both the base and the superstructure would differ in each major phase of development—from slave society to feudalism and feudalism to capitalism.

Economic development took place during each of these phases, but ultimately such development created tensions. For example, while technological advances and improved communications (that is, progress in the material productive forces) had made it possible for capitalism to develop during the stage of feudalism, the traditional systems of landownership and taxation had inhibited those developments. Such tensions led to conflicts between the existing feudal structure and the embryonic capitalist (bourgeois) one. These were expressed through political and ideological clashes, culminating in social revolution. Following this, the capitalist economic structure became dominant, leading to new social relations and a superstructure conducive to its further development. However, in this latest era economic development had been so successful that it would now be possible to establish a socialist society without the fundamental antagonisms that had characterized the previous phases of development. Capitalism brought 'the prehistory of human society to a close'.

This passage encapsulates very important parts of Marxist theory, but there are controversies about its main contentions. In particular, it implies that the base entirely determines the superstructure, but other passages in the works of Marx and Engels are much less categorical, and there have also been disputes within Marxist circles about how the relationship operates. Many have argued that ideas and institutions may have far more influence on the base than the Preface implies, and also that the whole idea of 'stages of development' is too rigid and mechanistic. Finally, as I discuss later, the meaning of social revolution has been highly controversial.

For socialists, the most important part of the theory was the critique of capitalism itself and the basis for confidence about its eventual downfall. Again, the theory operated on a number of levels. In *The Communist Manifesto*, Marx and Engels suggested that there were only two antagonistic classes at the heart of the system:

> Our epoch, the epoch of the bourgeoisie, possesses . . . this distinctive feature: it has simplified the class antagonisms. Society as a whole is more and more splitting up into two great hostile camps, into two great classes directly facing each other: Bourgeoisie [capitalist class] and Proletariat [working class].

This suggested that all other groups (landowners, peasants, artisans) were being squeezed into one or other of these classes. Marx was not always so categorical about this, but certainly argued that it was the contradictory economic interests of these two classes that contained the seeds of destruction of the system.

The starting point for the analysis was a theory of classical political economy: the labour theory of value. The argument here was that the amount of labour necessary to produce a particular product constituted its value. Labour value thus differed from exchange value or price. Marx began with this theory and also thought that in pre-capitalist societies products had been exchanged because they were useful to the people who bought them. However, he noted that this was not what happened under capitalism: here the point was to produce commodities that could be exchanged for money and profit. Furthermore, labour (which he now called 'labour power') had also become a commodity to be bought and sold, but its exchange value was not as great as the exchange value of the product it created. This led Marx to introduce the concept of *surplus value*.

Put simply, his argument was as follows. Those who owned capital, which was transformed into the means of production (e.g. factories, raw materials, machinery), sought profit by producing commodities for sale in the market. This kind of capital did not change its value during the production process. However, labour power did change value. First, it was able to produce the equivalent of its own value, which, Marx assumed, was normally subsistence for the labourer and their family. For example, if this was £50 per day, the worker might perhaps produce goods of such value within the first four working hours. However, by working for another four hours each day, the labourer could produce double the value (that is, another £50).

This would mean that £100 of value had been produced, and the excess between subsistence and the amount taken by capitalists would be the *surplus value* (in this case £50). Profits came from surplus value, but some expenditure—for example, on new machinery—would also be taken from it. The fundamental economic struggle between labour and capital was over the *rate of surplus value* (which Marx also called the 'rate of exploitation'), with owners of the means of production wanting to increase it and workers to reduce it through higher wages. This meant that the capitalist system was prone to crisis.

If labour power produced surplus value, and therefore profit, there were persistent problems at the heart of the system. Individual capitalists would need to modernize their systems of production through improvements in machinery and technology so as to compete with their rivals. But this meant that they would want to increase their investment in machinery at the expense of labour, which would therefore mean that the share going to labour would decline. However, since only labour power generated surplus value there was a long-term tendency for this to fall. Increasing either the hours of work or the productivity of labour through new technology could offset the immediate problems. But, in Marx's view, these were only temporary expedients. Improved production methods meant that more commodities reached the market, but capitalists still needed to keep wages down so as to derive surplus value from each worker. Yet this meant that labour would not have the purchasing power to buy the additional goods and, in this case, production could no longer be profitable.

The system would therefore face a crisis of overproduction leading to two results. First, there would be a period of takeovers and mergers as the strongest enterprises forced competitors out of business and effectively destroyed some of the means of production. Second, there would be a depression of wages and the creation of mass unemployment, with increasing poverty and suffering for the proletariat. Eventually, this would lead to a new phase of production in which further capital accumulation based on profits derived from surplus value would again be possible; but the same structural problems would remain, and new crises were endemic in capitalism. Moreover, each crisis would tend to be more severe than the previous one, eventually leading to the breakdown of the system itself.

Marx appeared to be saying something very categorical: that the position of the proletariat was becoming ever more wretched and that the downfall of capitalism was inevitable. In fact, he may have been less certain about the absolute decline in working-class living standards than it appeared. He also believed that trade unionism and reforms could lead to definite improvements in the situation of the workers and that 'subsistence' was a historical concept, so that its meaning would be affected by changing conceptions of the minimum acceptable standard of living as society evolved. Similarly, despite rhetoric that sometimes implied that the collapse of capitalism was imminent, elsewhere he suggested that it would take a very long time to exhaust all its possibilities of expansion. Yet the notion of eventual breakdown was embedded in both Marx's materialist conception of history and his political economy of capitalism.

The seeds of transformation were inherent within the operation of the existing system, which was never static. The future was not to be created by establishing communities practising a new system, as the utopian socialists had believed, or by a group of people 'smashing the state', as in some anarchist visions. Nor, however, did Marx believe that structural forces determined everything. On the contrary, political activity by the proletariat was essential, for its growing class consciousness would also bring about a developing awareness of the bourgeoisie as both separate and antagonistic. From this, socialist and revolutionary consciousness would also emerge over time. Thus the structural features of capitalism created an objective antagonism between the two fundamental classes within it; but the development and operation of the system then produced a subjective consciousness that would ultimately lead to a revolutionary process, focusing on the capture of state power.

This followed from Marx and Engels's theory of the origins of the state. This, they argued, had developed only with the earliest division of labour, which had arisen once society had been able to produce a surplus that some people could live off without contributing directly to producing the means of life for the whole community. Subsequently, the state had primarily been an instrument to serve the interests of the dominant class in each social system. The *Communist Manifesto* asserted that 'the executive of the modern state is but a committee for managing the common affairs of the whole bourgeoisie'. This overstated Marx and Engels's position, but expressed the essence of their theory. Nevertheless, there has been considerable debate in Marxist circles about the exact relationship between society and the state, with many arguing that it has far more autonomy than the above formulation suggests.

The emphasis of Marx's writings and speeches suggested that revolutionary change would involve violence. Yet he was also critical of those who equated revolution with insurrection or a coup by an organized group. Marx's point was that a revolutionary crisis was the culmination of a much longer evolutionary process within the existing society. This meant that a premature attempt to bring about a revolution could not succeed, and he criticized the violence of the most radical elements (the Jacobins) in the French Revolution, arguing that their failure followed from the attempt to impose conditions for which society was not yet ready. In 1848, and at the time of the Paris Commune in 1871, he appeared to accept the need for violence, but at other times he urged the path of reform. He even held out the possibility of peaceful revolution, suggesting that Britain, the USA, and Holland might possess the appropriate conditions for this to take place. After Marx's death, Engels seemed more decided on this path, working with the German Sozialdemokratische Partei Deutschlands (SPD) on practical programmes for reform.

Social democracy before 1914

By 1883, when Marx died, the major features of socialist ideas had been established. Utopian socialists, anarchists, and Marxists had many crucial points of disagreement, but there was a common emphasis on equality, cooperation, and social solidarity. All also stressed their commitment to the poorer social strata, although it was only with Marx that a specific theory of class and class conflict had crystallized. After his death the final forms of modern socialism emerged, with the dominance of political parties.

Between the 1880s and the outbreak of the First World War, there was a massive growth in socialist parties in Europe, all of which came together in the Second International, founded in 1889. Their names, confusing at the time, have become much more so in the light of later developments. For although they were collectively known as socialist parties when meeting in the International, and most of them professed the goal of socialism, only a minority used the term in their own names. Some used 'workers' or 'labour', but the most common title was 'social democratic party'. Communist parties did not yet exist and social democracy covered a spectrum of views, including those that would later identify themselves with communism.

With the British Labour Party as the only important exception, the parties owed their doctrinal inspiration mainly to the Marxist critique of capitalism. The SPD in Germany was easily the largest party in the International and the most dominant intellectually. During these years, Karl Kautsky (1854–1938) became the most influential interpreter of Marxist doctrine, not only in the German Social Democratic Party, but in the International as a whole. Having lived in London for much of the 1880s, he became quite close to Engels and this reinforced his credentials as the authentic voice of Marxism. However, he tended to interpret the theory in a rather mechanical way, emphasizing the inevitability of the eventual triumph of socialism. His position also epitomized the difficulties of attempting to reconcile a revolutionary doctrine with electoral and parliamentary politics. It incorporated the key tensions between reform and revolution that characterized the International as a whole.

The SPD's programme was agreed at Erfurt in 1891 and, as Donald Sassoon has argued, two aspects coexisted within it, with rather tenuous links between them. The first part was an orthodox Marxist summary of the situation, stressing the division of society into two hostile camps, with diminishing numbers of large-scale capitalist enterprises constantly expanding their control over the economic system, ever more serious crises of overproduction, and the necessity for the SPD to acquire political power so as to establish a socialist system based on common ownership. The second part concentrated on a series of measures that appeared to constitute a programme of reform within the system, rather than its total transformation. Despite different shades of opinion within the party, most regarded it as a programme that combined immediate benefits for the proletariat with the long-term goal of socialism. In other words, it was generally seen as both a reformist and revolutionary programme, with reforms sought within capitalism—not as a *substitute* for revolution, but as a *means* towards it. This was the dominant interpretation within the SPD and more widely within the Second International.

By 1914, the emergence of social democratic parties seeking mass membership and majority electoral support had already pushed alternative socialist traditions to the margins. This did not mean that there were no challengers. For example, in the years immediately before the war there was a sharp increase in militant rank-and-file strikes in several European countries. This reflected a belief (often defined as syndicalism) that direct industrial action, rather than working through political parties, was the way to achieve change and construct a new society. Yet this was now an alternative rather than a mainstream position.

One further element in the newly dominant tradition of socialism was its professed acceptance of working-class internationalism (see Figure 4). Following Marx and Engels, this held that the workers had no country because their common enemy was capitalism. Hence all the parties agreed, in theory, that they would be totally opposed to a capitalist war. None of them, it was constantly asserted, would support their own governments should such a war break out. In reality, most of them did just this in 1914. This greatly increased the divisions within the parties, with an active minority opposing both the mainstream leadership and the war. Yet it might have been possible to reconstruct the International after the war had it not been for the Bolshevik (communist) Revolution in 1917.

The emergence of communism

The assumption of power in Russia by the Bolshevik Party created modern communism. Subsequently, the new rulers claimed that the party represented the authentic application of Marxism in the contemporary era, and implied that there was continuity between themselves and 19th-century communists. In fact, the relationship between Bolshevism and Marxism remains highly controversial and the idea of continuity is very dubious. There was no clear distinction between communism and socialism for most of the previous century. At times, the term communism had implied a more revolutionary approach to bringing about change, and this impression was perhaps reinforced with the publication of the *Communist Manifesto*. But the manifesto was written for the so-called Communist League, a group of émigré German workers that soon faded away, and the terms 'socialist' and 'communist' were not even used consistently by Marx and Engels.

4. This lithograph of the Second International by the artist Theophile-Alexandre Steinlen (1858–1923) provided him with an opportunity to demonstrate his socialist beliefs.

According to all the guardians of orthodoxy, Russia should not have been the location for the first Marxist-inspired revolution, for the peasantry formed the overwhelming majority of the population and serfdom was only abolished in 1861. In general,

Marx and Engels had emphasized the argument that the revolution would first occur in an advanced capitalist country, although Marx himself was becoming more open-minded about this at the end of his life. Until 1914, Russian Marxists generally shared the orthodox view and tended to defer to Kautsky, the main theorist of the German SPD, on many issues of doctrine. However, earlier developments in the Russian party, along with the crisis over the war, now combined to transform the situation.

The Russian Social-Democratic Labour Party was formed in 1899 as the main organizational focus for Russian Marxists, but it soon dissolved into factions, one of which was led by Vladimir Lenin (1870–1924). Because of his energy, clarity, and revolutionary commitment, he soon emerged as a leading figure, and, in *What is to be Done?* (1902), he proposed the establishment of a wholly new type of party. This brought about a split the following year, with Lenin's Bolsheviks (meaning 'majority') now operating as a separate party before a final break in 1912.

Subsequently, Lenin totally opposed socialists in any part of the world who supported the First World War and sought (unsuccessfully) to persuade dissident socialists to turn the war into a revolutionary struggle in their own countries. The Bolshevik seizure of power in October 1917 (which later became November with a change in the calendar) transformed the power relationships within the international socialist movement. With a change of the party's name, from 'Bolshevik' to 'Communist', Moscow became the centre of the international communist movement.

The situation in Russia at the time of the revolution was highly complex. In 1905 there had already been a revolutionary attempt in which Soviets (workers' councils) were formed. The government quelled this wave of popular protest with a mixture of extreme repression and reforms, but in 1917 new Soviets of soldiers and workers were established in the major cities, particularly Petrograd (now St Petersburg). In February (March after the calendar change) a combination of strikes, protests over bread shortages, and mutinies by some army units brought about the abdication of the tsar. A new government was formed, but the allies persuaded it to continue with the war, although this was a major cause of popular unrest.

Most Bolsheviks still believed that it was impossible for a socialist revolution to take place in an overwhelmingly peasant country, but Lenin now returned from exile in Switzerland and convinced them that a revolutionary attempt could succeed in Russia and would be followed elsewhere. The hope was that like-minded governments in more advanced countries would then help the development of socialism in Russia. With the slogans of 'all power to the Soviets' and 'bread, land and peace', the Bolsheviks secured a majority in the Soviets and achieved a revolutionary insurrection. This enabled the party to take control because there was currently a power vacuum between a weak provisional government on the one hand and the active Soviets on the other.

Shortly before the seizure of power, Lenin wrote *The State and Revolution* (1917), which was wildly optimistic about the way in which socialism could be established after a revolution. The reality was quite different, for the Bolsheviks were now faced with four tasks that were not easily reconcilable. First, they had to establish themselves in power when they had only a minority of support in the predominantly rural country. Second, they needed to implement measures that would demonstrably change social relationships in a rigidly authoritarian society based on traditional hierarchies. Third, they needed to maintain the temporary alliance between the peasantry and the urban proletariat that had enabled them to seize control. Fourth, they needed to bring about massive economic growth so as to improve living standards. It is perhaps hardly surprising that they failed, particularly as their more positive aims were necessarily subordinated, until the end of 1920, to the urgent task of winning a civil war.

Even after taking power, the party talked of a democratically elected Constituent Assembly as the body that would rule, and it clearly expected to win a majority there. However, when the election results in January 1918 showed that the communists had won only 21 per cent of the seats, they dissolved the Assembly. As far as Lenin was concerned, the situation by then was such that the only alternatives were communist rule or rule by the extreme right, and he was not willing to risk the latter.

His analysis of the situation was probably valid, but the decision obviously had important political implications. It soon led to a situation in which the communists dominated all organs of power and, by the end of the civil war, the party and the Red Army had become increasingly autocratic. Each new extension of power was justified as a temporary measure, but a party/state dictatorship was now being constructed.

As early as December 1917, the Cheka (or secret police) was established to discover and suppress any attempts at counter-revolution. It used summary executions and imprisonment against suspects—some of whom were regarded as such simply because of their social origins. After an attempt on Lenin's life in May 1918, the Red Terror was promulgated, leading to thousands of executions and the Cheka operating almost as a state within the state. Furthermore, by 1920 the economy was destitute after six years of war, peasant support for the revolution was eroding, and some eight million people had died from disease and malnutrition.

The break between communism and social democracy

While many European socialists were exhilarated by the first Marxist-inspired revolution, others were less convinced. As they watched the dissolution of the Constituent Assembly, the revolutionary terror, and the evolution towards a one-party state, their doubts as to whether this was really socialism increased. In some cases, particularly amongst the leaders of West European socialist parties, such sentiments were probably reinforced when they heard themselves denounced as traitors and renegades by the Soviet leaders. Other Western socialists were prepared to accept that such harsh measures might be necessary in Russian conditions, where there had been no tradition of democracy and where counter-revolutionaries also used terror as a political weapon, but not in countries where peaceful change through constitutional means might be possible. Others went further than this and questioned whether the Bolshevik Revolution could even be justified in Marxist terms. One of the most powerful arguments of this kind was put forward in December 1920 at a Congress of the French Socialist Party in Tours.

The Congress was held to decide whether or not the party should affiliate to the new Communist International. Léon Blum (1872–1950), who would become Prime Minister in the French Popular Front government in 1936, was the leader of one of the groups totally opposed to affiliation. In his speech, he claimed that the dictatorship in Russia stemmed from its conception of revolution. Instead of a seizure of power following a long period of evolution creating the preconditions for socialism, the Bolsheviks had interpreted revolution as an insurrection by a small group, who then needed to create those preconditions. Whereas the Marxist conception was of a temporary impersonal dictatorship based on mass support, the Bolshevik one was of semi-permanent dictatorship exercised by a centralized and hierarchical party. Blum was thus implying either that socialism could not be established in this way, or that the only form that could emerge would negate its own ideals because it was inherently undemocratic. However, he was defeated at the Congress, and the majority now formed the French Communist Party.

The fissure that opened up between communism and social democracy developed in the aftermath of the Bolshevik

Revolution, but some relevant aspects of Lenin's thinking had been revealed even before 1914 and these were now institutionalized. The most fundamental element was his absolute commitment to the goal of socialist revolution. This underlay his whole strategic and tactical approach, including important innovations. For example, most Marxists had tended to regard the urban working class as the vehicle for socialist revolution and were often rather indifferent both to the peasantry and to the forces of nationalism. However, Lenin had understood that a revolution could take place in Russia only on the basis of alliances with the peasantry and the numerous subject nationalities that sought liberation from rule by the Russian majority. But it was his belief in the necessity for a particular kind of party to hasten the revolutionary process that was of particular relevance for the subsequent split with social democracy.

His idea of a vanguard party, based on revolutionaries fighting a class war in the same way as the military fought a conventional one, differed from anything suggested by Marx and Engels. They had taken it for granted that a party would be necessary, but had also insisted that the working class would emancipate itself. However, Lenin argued that, left to itself, the working class would develop 'trade union' consciousness, but not revolutionary consciousness. In other words, conflicts over pay and working conditions would inevitably arise, but the workers would not themselves locate these issues within a wider Marxist framework. Because they remained integrated within the dominant ideological assumptions, it was necessary for a vanguard party to bring revolutionary socialist consciousness to them. This was an extremely contentious notion.

Lenin might argue that this was not party control *over* the workers because it would be working *with* them, but there were certainly elements of elitism in this view. For it suggested that workers had a 'false consciousness' that must be redirected by those with superior understanding. The serious implications of this notion were reinforced by Lenin's ideas about party organization, for all the emphasis was upon secrecy, centralization, and professional revolutionaries. Some of his thinking was certainly shaped by the need to operate in clandestine conditions during the tsarist autocracy, which he contrasted with the relatively open conditions in Germany. Yet he slid from a discussion about the Russian situation to far more general notions, which implied that centralism and secrecy were more important to him than democracy. Furthermore, the very idea of a party leadership having the right to impose a single view on its members was highly questionable. The result was likely to be one in which policy directives became diktats, with most members simply having to take it on trust that decisions had been arrived at through discussion and debate. This was compounded by the fact that the party's message under Lenin was always based on binary alternatives: a given idea or policy was *either* bourgeois *or* socialist—shades of grey did not exist.

Although many commentators have tended to regard the Leninist party as pivotal for the subsequent establishment of the dictatorship by Stalin (1879–1953), it can equally well be argued that Stalin destroyed and bypassed it. Many revolutionary Marxists, who are highly critical of the direction taken by the Soviet Union, therefore continue to believe that the Leninist conception of the party, based on the system of 'democratic centralism', was valid and the problems only developed with later applications of that conception. Yet it is notable that two of the most eminent Marxist revolutionaries of the era had also criticized Lenin's notion of the vanguard party when it had first been formulated.

Rosa Luxemburg (1871–1919) was a revolutionary Marxist in the German SPD. She was deeply critical of the leadership of her own party, regarding it as too dominated by short-term reforms and losing sight of the ultimate goal of socialist revolution. She believed in mass action by the working class as the way of bringing about change and was critical of Lenin's concept of a vanguard party. In 1904, she attacked it for ultra-centralism, which she equated with the 'sterile spirit of the overseer':

> Lenin's concern is not so much to make the activity of the party more fruitful as to control the party—to narrow the movement rather than to develop it, to bind rather than unify it.

Once the Russian Revolution took place, she gave it cautious support and was a leading figure in the German Communist Party when it was established in December 1918. However, the next month she was arrested by German cavalry officers, who were suppressing a revolutionary uprising, and murdered while in custody.

The other early critic was Leon Trotsky (1879–1940). When Lenin developed his concept of the party, Trotsky had not supported him, but he subsequently changed his mind and became a leading figure in the revolution of 1917 and the post-revolutionary regime. When Lenin died in January 1924, Trotsky was one of the two most probable successors, but he was outmanoeuvred by Stalin, who expelled him from the Soviet Union in 1929. In exile, he denounced the betrayal of revolution and sought to revive the original spirit of Bolshevism as he interpreted it. As a result, Stalin's agents in Mexico assassinated him in 1940.

Trotsky always insisted that there was no basis for Stalinism in Lenin's concept of the party, and subsequently Trotskyist parties and movements have generally taken this view. However, his initial verdict on the idea could be taken as a prediction of the methods that Stalin would later use and from which Trotsky himself would suffer. In 1904 he thus wrote:

> In inner-party politics, these methods [of Lenin] lead, as we shall yet see, to this: the party organisation substitutes itself for the party, the Central Committee substitutes itself for the organisation and, finally, a 'dictator' substitutes himself for the Central Committee.

The origins of Bolshevik Party organization lay in Russian conditions, but by 1919 the situation had been transformed. Convinced that a revolution could occur elsewhere if the organizational and ideological features of Bolshevism were adopted, the model was now imposed on all parties seeking to join the new Communist International (the Comintern) created in Moscow. The entry conditions required all who joined to accept the doctrine and practices of the Bolsheviks in their own parties, with the Comintern largely determining the policies of the individual parties. This notion of a centrally controlled, vanguard revolutionary party was distasteful to socialists who believed in reform and democracy. Thus when the Comintern insisted that this model must be imposed on all member parties, the break with social democracy was clear.

Yet it would be wrong to attribute responsibility for this entirely to Soviet communism, for the Marxist terminology of Second International socialism had masked a tendency that now became much stronger: the pursuit of socialism through constitutional means. Before the war, only the British Labour Party had explicitly avowed constitutional politics as the sole means to bring about change, and it had also concentrated on practical reforms rather than discussions of ultimate goals. Elsewhere, while the official claim that reforms were just one element in a Marxist revolutionary strategy had survived intact until 1914, the support for the war had exposed the gap between rhetoric and reality.

The performance of some of the parties after the fighting ended confirmed the view that working within the system would supersede any previous claims that the objective was to overthrow it through extra-parliamentary activity. The most notorious instance of this was the SPD's collaboration with the old elites to establish the Weimar Republic in 1919 rather than to support those who were attempting to overthrow capitalism through revolution. It is highly unlikely that a revolution could have succeeded, but the caution of the SPD leadership was widely criticized both at the time and subsequently. Its reliance on paramilitary forces made the break between social democracy and communism particularly bitter in Germany. However, the more general point is that after 1920 a new form of social democracy emerged that effectively abandoned the idea of seeking socialism through a revolutionary seizure of power.

Many parties still used Marxist terminology and attempted to justify their policies in relation to the ultimate goal of revolution. Some breakaway parties even fought bravely to find a 'third way' between communism and social democracy in the so-called Vienna International established in 1921. However, they abandoned this attempt in 1923, when the Labour and Socialist International was established. This concentrated primarily on seeking power through parliamentary means and advocating practical reforms, with the British Labour Party entering the mainstream of social democracy. There was now an absolute division between social democracy and communism.

The Communists were institutionally part of the Comintern and sought to emulate Soviet theory and practice. Social democrats rejected the Soviet model and effectively accepted the notion that there was *some* convergence between their own views and those of others, such as left-wing liberals, who believed in parliamentary democracy and social reform. Two kinds of political parties, allegedly serving the interests of the working classes, had become the main agencies for the establishment of socialism, and these two traditions now struggled for ascendancy in Europe and the rest of the world.

Chapter 2
Cuban communism and Swedish social democracy

Developments in communism and social democracy

The fissure between communism and social democracy that developed in the aftermath of the Bolshevik Revolution never really healed, although neither tradition was monolithic or unchanging.

In general, social democratic parties experienced persistent difficulties in self-definition after the break with communism. Most of them had claimed to be Marxist before 1914, and disputed the communist appropriation of the doctrine in the early post-war period. On the other hand, they generally accepted liberal democratic institutions as the primary route through which to implement changes. Some parties continued to claim Marxism as a doctrinal source long after it ceased to play an important role in influencing their policies. The French Socialist Party was particularly prone to this. Thus Léon Blum, still facing the pre-1914 problem as to whether a socialist party could participate in a bourgeois coalition, distinguished between 'the exercise of power' (participation in government) and 'the conquest of power' (overthrow of capitalism). Yet although his Popular Front government in 1936 implemented some important reforms immediately after coming to power, its subsequent economic policy was unimaginative and non-socialist.

In Germany, the situation of the SPD was to become more catastrophic. Despite its pre-eminent role in establishing the liberal-democratic system in 1919 and remaining committed to it during the years of acute instability until 1923, the party was then normally excluded from power by coalitions of other parties, although it secured the largest share of the vote until 1930. In 1928 the SPD's success in the elections meant that no cabinet could be formed without it, but it would not agree to the cut in unemployment benefit sought by its partners. The result was the effective abolition of the parliamentary system and rule by decree from 1930. The bitter division between the SPD and the Communist Party then prevented a united front against Nazism, though both parties were immediate victims after Hitler's takeover of power in 1933. The SPD had wanted to uphold the democratic system and remained committed to constitutionalism even when it was increasingly evident that its opponents supported dictatorship. But it never formulated a programme of reform to resolve the economic crisis after 1929, tending to share the communist belief that this was the final collapse of capitalism. The SPD represented inter-war social democracy in its most tragic form.

Yet the difficulties were not confined to the parties that still claimed a Marxist influence. Neither of the brief attempts of the British Labour Party to wield power through minority governments in the inter-war period was notably successful. In particular, its failure to deal with the economic depression in 1931, and the decision of its leader and then prime minister, Ramsay MacDonald (1866–1937), to head a Conservative-dominated coalition in order to implement austerity measures, led to the worst crisis the party faced until 2019. Confined to opposition for the rest of the inter-war period, it was divided and relatively impotent until it joined the wartime coalition led by Winston Churchill.

The *raison d'être* of social democracy after the split with communism was the claim that socialism could be implemented peacefully. However, with the notable exception of the Nordic countries, particularly Sweden, the general experience of the inter-war period was one of failure. Most capitalist societies experienced either serious economic depression, characterized by mass unemployment and a reduction in social expenditure, or, still worse, the elimination of liberal-democracy and its replacement by extreme right-wing dictatorship. Such outcomes clearly constituted a practical and intellectual defeat for the project of social democracy. For it had manifestly failed to eliminate poverty and create a more equal society imbued with the values of cooperation and solidarity. Subsequently, both the nature of social democracy and the problems it faced underwent further changes.

During the inter-war period, the only large liberal-democratic country that successfully implemented *practical* measures to revive the economy and create jobs was the USA, under President Roosevelt and the New Deal. However, Roosevelt was not a socialist, but a pragmatic American Democrat. Similarly, the foremost economist, who explained *in theoretical terms* how a government could stimulate economic expansion during a depression, was John Maynard Keynes (1883–1946), a British Liberal. So neither the practical nor the theoretical originators of the reforms underlying post-war capitalism were from the social democratic tradition. When 'Keynesian' economics was put into practice between the late 1940s and the early 1970s, there was a prolonged period of economic growth, leading to far higher living standards in Western Europe, and a much greater proportion of Gross National Produce (GNP) devoted to welfare expenditure than ever before. This new era of the so-called 'welfare state', where governments assumed a major responsibility for the social and economic well-being of citizens, raised new questions for social democracy and a further evolution.

As social expenditure increased and full employment was established, most social democratic parties now became more openly committed to the goal of progressive social reform, rather than the total elimination of the capitalist system. This was not a smooth or uniform process, for the parties contained minorities that adhered to a more traditional version of socialism. Some parties even insisted that they had not changed. Certainly, important differences remained between them, with variations in ideology, relationships with trade unions, and the social composition of the members and supporters of the parties. Yet social democracy could now be characterized as a tradition seeking to promote increasing benefits for the working classes within a primarily capitalist system. The fact that control over much of the economy remained in private hands inevitably limited the power of social democracy and further constraints stemmed from its need to secure electoral support for its measures.

Communism also evolved after the break with social democracy. After 1917, communist parties were established throughout the world but, until the end of the Second World War, communism was inseparable from the experience in the Soviet Union. For it was only there that a communist regime was in power, and the other parties demonstrated their allegiance to it. Soviet dominance was then reinforced with the establishment in the 1940s of a communist bloc in East Central Europe under its control. But the leader of Yugoslavia, Josip Broz Tito (1892–1980), had a serious dispute with Stalin, breaking away from the bloc in 1948. Tito's system was also based on one-party rule, but with far greater decentralization of the economy than in the Soviet Union. Of greater importance, in 1949 the Chinese Communist Party under Mao Zedong (1893–1976) finally achieved power after more than twenty years of revolutionary struggle and civil war. The Chinese system differed considerably from the Soviet model, with much more emphasis on the continuing role of the peasantry. Furthermore, by the 1960s relations between China and the Soviet Union had become so poor that border clashes took place and a war seemed possible. This also led to divisions within the international communist movement, with some now turning to Maoism for their inspiration. Other communist regimes were also established: in North Korea, following a division in the country after the Second World War; in Vietnam (initially in the north of the country, but throughout the whole state in 1975 following the withdrawal of the USA after a prolonged war); and in Cuba, after the revolution in 1959.

Greater diversity in communism also followed from revelations made by the Soviet leader Nikita Khrushchev (1894–1971) at the party congress in 1956. There he denounced aspects of Stalin's rule, presenting some of the evidence about the atrocities that had taken place. This led some West European communist parties (particularly those in Italy and Spain) gradually to move away from Soviet control and, during the 1970s, to proclaim the doctrine of 'Eurocommunism'. In this they declared their acceptance of a multi-party system, free speech, and many characteristics of liberal democracy. But, despite their many differences, all communist states maintained a single-party system, substantial state ownership of the economy, an adherence to an official ideology based on an interpretation of Marxism, and the maintenance of power through non-democratic means.

Commentary on both communism and social democracy has tended to be dominated by a concentration upon the biggest powers: the Soviet Union and China in relation to communism; and Germany, Britain, and France in relation to social democracy. While this is understandable in the sense that the big battalions dominate world history, it can also lead to unjustifiably negative conclusions about socialism. This is particularly obvious in respect of the Soviet Union and China, where the scale of violence and repression makes it difficult to scrutinize the costs and benefits of the regimes dispassionately. The failings of social democratic governments within the large European states bear no comparison with the crimes of Stalinism or Maoism, but it is difficult to argue that they ever created an alternative model of society reflecting socialist values.

While no party has been entirely successful in this respect, Swedish social democracy and Cuban communism both attempted to implement the goals of equality, cooperation, and solidarity and both demonstrated significant achievements. I have selected these two states as case studies for this reason.

Presenting these case studies side by side does not imply symmetry between them. The important differences between communism and social democracy that emerged after the Bolshevik Revolution affected the ideological universe of each, particularly in relation to such key issues as democracy and private ownership. The environments in which they operated were also quite different. In 1959 (the year of the Cuban revolution) Swedish social democrats had the comparative luxury of living in a wealthy and stable liberal-democracy facing no significant external threat, while the dominating preoccupations for Fidel Castro were the poverty of the island and its extreme vulnerability to attack by the bitterly hostile superpower just across the water. Nevertheless, there are also some interesting points of comparison, for both Swedish social democrats and Cuban communists tried to bring about significant social changes in a world dominated by much larger powers, and both became increasingly constrained by changes in the wider international political economy.

Swedish social democracy

The Swedish Social Democratic Party (Socialdemokratiska Arbetarpartiet, or SAP) paid formal obeisance to Marxism before 1914, but there were some strongly revisionist overtones in both its rhetoric and formal statements even then. Hjalmar Branting, who dominated the party from 1900 until 1925, was originally a liberal and, particularly in his later years, sought to effect a synthesis between liberalism and socialism. Another important figure, Per Albin Hansson, who became the first SAP prime minister in 1932, made a frequently quoted statement that characterized a further key aspect in Swedish social democracy— the *folkhemmet*, or conception of society and the state as the 'people's home':

> The basis of the home is togetherness and common feeling. The good house does not consider anyone either as privileged or unappreciated; it knows no special favourites and no stepchildren. There no one looks down upon anyone else, there no one tries to gain advantage at another's expense, and the stronger do not suppress and plunder the weaker. In the good home equality, consideration, co-operation and helpfulness prevail. Applied to the great people's and citizens' home this would mean the breaking down of all the social and economic barriers that now divide citizens into the privileged and the unfortunate, into rulers and subjects . . .

In its unbroken period of rule from 1932 until 1976 (except for a very brief period in 1936), the SAP introduced a series of major and enduring economic and social reforms broadly in harmony with these sentiments.

A further characteristic of Swedish social democracy was the fact that it rested as much on trade unionism, and particularly the blue-collar confederation, the Landsorganisationen (LO), as on the party. This was not unique to Sweden, for there was also an organic relationship between British trade unionism and the Labour Party. However, in the Swedish case, the power of the central confederation over other unions meant that policy was normally hammered out between the SAP and the LO. This was related to another key feature—the intellectual rigour of many of the proposals and policies, which were as often the creation of the

LO as the SAP. Whereas some of the most creative policy proposals in other countries came from figures outside social democracy—for example, John Maynard Keynes—in Sweden they tended to come from the mainstream of the movement. Thus Ernest Wigforss had already devised a counter-cyclical economic policy so as to stimulate demand and reduce unemployment (anticipating Keynes's *General Theory*), before becoming minister of finance. Holding this position from 1932 until 1949, he then had the power to implement some of his strategies. Similarly, the eminent social economists Gunnar and Alva Myrdal (1898–1987; 1902–86) were within the social democratic 'establishment' and this facilitated acceptance of their pioneering ideas in social policy in the 1930s.

Although the SAP governments did not always proceed as quickly or as radically as some of their supporters hoped, they constantly sought to advance further in relation to the goals of equality and solidarity. Thus at the end of the 1980s, Sweden remained the Western society with the highest percentage of Gross Domestic Product (GDP) devoted to health, education, and related programmes. Moreover, various studies in the 1970s and 1980s showed that redistribution continued to be greater in Sweden than in any other country, even though it had the lowest rate of inequality at the beginning of the period of analysis.

Some of the significant gains in equality were side effects of other policies, in particular, to the demand for labour in an era of economic expansion. Thus the female participation rate for all women rose from 51 per cent in 1960 to 76.9 per cent in 1980, and a comparative study of twelve advanced capitalist states showed that in both years these employment rates were the highest. The participation rate for married women in 1980 was particularly notable, for in Sweden by then this was 75.6 per cent, with the second highest level (in the UK) at 57.2 per cent. In most countries, women employees were then confined to the low-paid sector, but in Sweden, because of the general trade union policies of increasing wages in the lowest-paid jobs and of equal pay for equal work, women gained greater protection than elsewhere. Neither this, nor the rapid expansion of nurseries and childcare centres, necessarily originated either in the commitment to sexual equality or even from social (rather than economic) policy.

As Chapter 3 will show, the relationships between feminism and socialism are complex and involve far more than work-related issues, and in Sweden the role of women's movements was crucial in broadening the conceptions of sexual equality that had originated in the demands of the economy. This relates to a wider point about Swedish social democracy: the way in which it became self-reinforcing as different groups secured a stake in its development.

Tim Tilton has argued that five central themes characterized Swedish social democracy. First, was *integrative democracy*, with democratic decision-making as the ultimate standard of legitimacy. The SAP was always committed to creating a society where industrial workers (and later employees as a whole) participated on equal terms in the organization and governance of society, but consensual rule remained the strong preference. This was related to the second element, the concept of the *'people's home'*, discussed above, with goals of solidarity and equality of treatment. Third, the SAP always argued that *socioeconomic equality and economic efficiency* were complementary rather than contradictory goals, and this was also closely connected to the fourth point—the pursuit of a *socially controlled market economy*, rather than nationalization. During the 1920s, the SAP abandoned the preoccupation with ownership and gradually adopted the notion of shifting the nature of markets through the distribution of income. Over time, this led to an emphasis on bargains with industrialists, with a gradual paring away of the prerogatives of capitalists through increasing social control.

The fifth theme was the belief that a *proper expansion of the public sector extended freedom of choice* by enhancing security for ordinary people. The dual assumptions were that the government was democratic and that taxation was not a threat to freedom, but a means of providing public services for the benefit of all. This led to public expenditure mounting to 60.1 per cent of GDP in 1980 in comparison with a mean average figure of 43.1 per cent for eighteen OECD countries, with social spending constituting 28.8 per cent of GDP in comparison with a mean average of 18.8 per cent with more than 30 per cent devoted to social services. However, marginal taxation rates were also higher than elsewhere for middle-income and managerial groups and by the end of the 1980s Sweden had the highest tax-to-GDP ratio in the world. This contributed to a backlash from the mid-1980s.

These themes constitute a general ideological outlook rather than a rigorous theory, but this shaped a whole gamut of policies. The same fundamental set of values of equality and solidarity underpinned the stance towards poorer countries, with Sweden consistently devoting one of the highest proportions of GNP to development aid. However, the success of social democracy also depended upon the extent to which its values shifted the nature of the society as a whole.

It would have been extremely difficult for the SAP to maintain power for so long had its policies been wholly unacceptable to the other parties and to other power-holders in society. It is notable that, even when there was a short interruption in its long period of office in 1976, there was no major break with the system that it had established and, in any case, it soon returned to government. There was therefore good reason to believe that society had now been reconstituted in the image of the SAP. One plausible argument for this proposition rested on the claim that social democracy was in harmony with some pre-existing aspects of Swedish society. Basic literacy was already comparatively high by the late 17th century, and the establishment of elementary schools after the mid-19th century furthered progress. This stress on education may have helped to foster both agricultural efficiency and a climate of debate. More generally, Henry Milner argued that Swedish political culture was characterised by values rooted in pre-industrial society: practical moderation, public spirit, equity, respect for individual autonomy, and a Lutheran attachment to the work ethic. Social democracy reinforced such values, and attitudinal surveys appeared to confirm Swedish pre-eminence in egalitarianism and the desire to resolve conflict through peaceful means.

Institutions and organizations reinforced the values. Sweden had the highest propensity for people to be involved in civic organizations of any country in the world. Most important of all, of course, was the fact that in the late 1980s the SAP itself had 1.2 million members (out of a total Swedish population of only 8.4 million). In addition to this, the country had the highest rate of unionization in the world. Not only was there the organic link between the LO and the SAP, but there was also a strong degree of support for it in the other trade union confederations, and in the cooperative movement, which had almost two million members and 90,000 employees. Finally, at their height, the SAP and LO had their own press and educational institutions and wielded considerable influence over a network of non-governmental organizations and popular movements.

Yet it is important not to exaggerate the long-term climate of tolerance. Favourable economic and political conditions may foster social attitudes emphasizing solidarity and equality, but major changes can also undermine such attitudes. Furthermore, there were always important limits on the *extent* of equality—set by the parameters of the private ownership system.

The success of social democracy remained dependent upon its ability to strike a bargain with its potential opponents. After all, even at the height of its post-war ascendancy, the SAP only once achieved 50 per cent of the vote (in 1968). It sometimes governed through a coalition (which it dominated) and it always needed the agreement of the business community. What, then, was the economic bargain that underpinned the Swedish model?

Its origins lay in an agreement in 1938 between the LO and the employers' organization, Svenska Arbetsgvarforeningen (SAF), but in 1951 two major economists, Gösta Rehn (1913–96) and Rudolf Meidner (1914–2005), reinforced the Swedish 'model' in a report submitted to the LO Congress. Before this, there had been a brief period of wage control and the Rehn–Meidner model was an alternative both to this kind of austerity and to the use of unemployment to curb wage demands. The government implemented this new model for the first time during a recession between 1957 and 1959.

The key to the approach was the belief that rising productivity was the essential precondition for increasing wages and financing the development of the welfare state. At the same time, Rehn and Meidner argued that the LO should coordinate wage bargaining so as to give support to the claims of the weakest unions. The originality of the model was that it identified the interests of those in a weak bargaining position with those of the labour movement as a whole. But the system rested on a wider agreement between the unions, the employers, and the government to support a regulated form of capitalism. A commitment to free trade exposed firms experiencing a profit squeeze to international competition so that they could not simply pass on higher wage costs to consumers. At the other end of the scale, the government would use taxation to limit the extent to which the more successful firms could use excessive profits to pay higher wages instead of investing in new capacity. The overall strategy therefore encouraged the concentration of capital, particularly of the large export-oriented firms, and the substitution of capital for labour.

The successful tripartite bargain between government, unions, and employers was the foundation for the Swedish welfare system. However, the bargain respected many of the prerogatives of management, and egalitarianism made little impact on some key aspects of inequality. For example, in the later 1970s, the top 0.1 per cent of shareholders held 25 per cent of share capital and the top 10 per cent held 75 per cent. All this would now become relevant as the pace of economic expansion declined and the threats to the Swedish model increased.

Pressures and problems

In the late 1960s there was some dissatisfaction in the labour movement with the practical results of the wage solidarity, which had led to the collapse of differentials in some sectors, while the most successful manufacturing companies were earning record profits. Greater union militancy brought about a series of important reforms, including in industrial democracy, but new proposals by the LO in 1976 precipitated a domestic reaction against the Swedish social model. The plan was for wage earners to take a progressively larger share of company capital as profits increased. This was a major step beyond the terms of the previous tripartite bargain and the employers mobilized against it in an unprecedented way, contributing to the loss of the 1976 election by the SAP.

The LO and SAP then worked together on a series of less radical versions of the project and, after the SAP returned to power in 1982, it implemented a diluted version of the plan in December 1983. But the setback was highly significant, for it reflected a long-term trend that would undermine Swedish social democracy in subsequent years. First, it suggested that the LO had gone beyond the employers' understanding of the limits of the bargain that had underpinned the 'model'. The SAF accepted moves towards greater industrial democracy, but would not tolerate the perceived threat to ownership. Second, the underlying economic and political situation was now beginning to change, favouring a new assertiveness by employers and centre and right-wing parties.

By the mid-1980s, the nature of the economy had shifted considerably. At the beginning of the decade the USA and the UK (under President Ronald Reagan and Margaret Thatcher) had launched a new era of 'neo-liberal' capitalism. This involved a dismantling of regulations, free movement of capital, privatization of nationalized enterprises, and the introduction of capitalist forms of organization into the public sector. With exports accounting for a high proportion of GNP and Swedish enterprises increasingly multinational, the economy was more exposed to international pressures than previously. The large exporters were also susceptible to the new international orthodoxies and by 1985 the government introduced considerable deregulation of the economy, followed by the ending of capital controls four years later. Entry into the European Union in 1995 was also very significant, for Sweden became subject to all the legislation and forms of economic integration that made it more difficult to preserve a distinctive system.

The economic changes had a major impact on the SAP and the LO. Blue-collar jobs were declining fast and between 1982 and 2014 their share in overall employment decreased from 20 per cent to 9 per cent. The shifting distribution of work undermined the pivotal position of the LO and in 1990 the most specific aspect of the Swedish model—the centralized bargaining system between the SAP and the SAF—collapsed. All this led to significant shifts in Swedish politics.

Above all, there was a decline in the SAP's dominance. Its massive membership had depended on collective trade union affiliations, but the LO now ceased this practice. By 1992 party membership declined to 250,000 and by 2017 it was just under 90,000. Until 1988 the party always secured well above 40 per cent of the vote, but subsequently it never reached these levels and in September 2018 its share declined to just over 28 per cent. There was also a marked decline in both class alignment and party loyalty. In 1982

70 per cent of the working classes voted for the SAP, but by 2018 only 31 per cent did so.

At the same time, there was some erosion of the network of support for the Swedish social model. Previously the majority of NGOs and social movements both upheld the social model and pressurized the government through campaigns and advocacy. But many civil society organizations evolved into professional providers of services, subject to contracts and new management systems. This also enhanced the role of business-oriented movements, and an emphasis on a contract culture and service delivery.

All these factors weakened the grip of the Social Democrats on government. The party was out of power between 1991 and 1994 and again between 2006 and 2014, after which it returned to head a rather insecure minority government in a 'Red–Green' coalition. After the September 2018 election, the situation remained so precarious that negotiations continued until late January when the SAP finally established an even more fragile minority coalition with the Green Party, with the parliamentary backing of the Centre and Liberal Parties.

In this more volatile situation, there was a very serious threat to the social and political consensus with the rise of extreme right-wing xenophobic movements. This was already visible in the 1990s when such a party gained nearly 7 per cent of the vote in 1991 before declining quickly. The problem then intensified when the Sweden Democrats (Sverigedemokraterna, SD) jettisoned an earlier overtly Nazi orientation and claimed to be a mainstream nationalist party. Their major opportunity came when Sweden, like Germany, adopted a liberal approach to migration from war zones, such as Syria and Afghanistan, and this, coupled with economic migration from poor countries, meant that by 2017 almost 19 per cent of Sweden's population came from abroad, with 11 per cent from Asia and Africa. With its anti-immigrant, nativist

Socialism

themes, the SD exploited these circumstances to challenge the political consensus, posing a major threat to social democracy, and securing 17.5 per cent of the popular vote in 2018. All the other parties, including the SAP, hardened their approach to migration in an attempt to undermine the appeal of the SD, although none of them would enter a coalition with it. Both this new threat, and the response to it, exposed the greater fragility of the social consensus and led to a rightward shift in political terms.

The end of an era?

All this leaves the question of whether Sweden is still a 'social democracy'. In the new international and domestic climate both SAP and centre-right governments have reduced taxes on inheritance, wealth, and residential properties, leading to a significant rise in inequality. Several analyses demonstrate a trend increase since the 1980s, with international comparisons showing Sweden in the top cluster of countries rather than in its former pre-eminent position. Similarly, the country is no longer at the top of the rankings on the percentage of GDP devoted to social expenditure and the changes are evident in various spheres of social policy. For example, educational inequalities rose quite sharply between 1998 and 2014.

Swedish social democracy had lost its shine, but it would also be premature to announce its death, for many important elements remained. Trade unionism maintains a more central role than in most countries. Blue-collar work may have declined, but the union confederations in the services and professional sectors have partially compensated for the reduction in the power of the LO and there is still a strong union relationship with the SAP. There is continuing strong support for the social welfare system and some aspects of social progress remain constant. In particular, while there is still gender inequality, the empowerment of women now seems to be an embedded feature of Swedish society. For example, a gender equality index for the EU at the end of 2017 showed that

Sweden was the most advanced throughout a ten-year period from 2005 and was continuing to make significant progress in 2018. The country has also played a leading international role in adapting to the urgency of the demands for climate change and environmental policy more generally. Nevertheless, its rate of progress in achieving the targets for greenhouse gas reduction slowed down and, as discussed in Chapter 3, it was in Sweden that the school student, Greta Thunberg, launched the international movement for school strikes to protest about the inadequate response to the threat of climate change.

There are also other parties that help to sustain support for social democracy. The alliance with the Green Party is generally helpful, although it became the smallest party in parliament after the 2018 election. The Left Party, which did comparatively well in 2018, with 8 per cent of the vote and twenty-eight parliamentary seats, continues to exert pressure in favour of the earlier social model.

Overall, therefore, Swedish social democracy is past its peak, but it retains considerable sources of strength. It has adapted to many features of the new forms of capitalism, while withstanding many of the pressures from an international climate that has become increasingly difficult for social democracy.

Cuban communism

Fidel Castro (1926–2016) assumed control of Cuban politics after a successful revolution in January 1959, and from the early 1960s progressively established a communist regime. The typical single-party/state system was created, and the country became closely aligned with the Soviet Union, with increasing economic dependence upon it after 1970. However, the nature of the initial revolution shaped many characteristics of the regime.

Ever since gaining independence from Spain in 1895, Cuban life had been marked by its economic dependency upon sugar, frequent military coups to prevent radical change, and US domination. This continued after the Second World War and in 1952 Fulgencio Batista launched a *coup d'état* supported by Washington.

The following year Fidel Castro, a 25-year-old law graduate, and his closest followers attempted to start a revolution by taking control of a military barracks. This failed and he was imprisoned, but released in a general amnesty two years later and then went into exile. Returning in December 1956, Castro's movement (named the 26 July movement, the date of the abortive insurrection in 1953) simultaneously built alliances with other groups and engaged in violent conflicts with the army. By late 1958, the Batista regime was finding it impossible to govern and the USA withdrew its support, hoping that it would be able to reach agreement with the revolutionary forces. Batista fled, and Castro's revolutionary movement assumed control (see Figure 5). The seizure of power was popular, but it was not yet clear what this implied.

The new government repudiated the past, showing a determination to renovate politics, and reject foreign intervention, while insisting that the rebel army would be the guarantor of the new Cuba. The main features of the initial programme were agrarian reform and progressive tax policies, which favoured Cuban over foreign investments, non-sugar over sugar sectors, small over large business, and the provinces over Havana. However, the apparently limited nature of the revolution was deceptive for two reasons: first, because of its social significance, and second, because of the centralization of power by Castro and his closest comrades.

In the late 1950s, Cuba was ranked among the top five countries in Latin America on a range of indicators, but over 40 per cent of the rural population were illiterate, fewer than 10 per cent of rural homes had electricity, and fewer than 3 per cent of rural

5. Revolutionary leader Fidel Castro waves to a cheering crowd upon his arrival in Havana, Cuba, after the dictator Fulgencio Batista fled the island.

households had indoor plumbing. There was widespread malnutrition and medical facilities were concentrated in Havana. The revolutionary regime concentrated on the poor and ordinary people. Land redistribution and the improvement of conditions on newly nationalized large farms had an immediate impact, and rent reductions transferred approximately 15 per cent of national income from property owners to wage workers and peasants.

At the same time, Castro strengthened his grip on power. He became prime minister in the middle of February 1959 and soon isolated his opponents. Revolutionary tribunals also judged and then executed some 500 members of Batista's police and security agents, and fears that this would continue led many of the propertied classes and non-revolutionary politicians into exile. Yet Castro also kept the Moscow-backed Popular Socialist Party (PSP) under control. The PSP had considerable experience in trade unionism, but Castro waited until the 26 July movement secured an overwhelming majority in the unions before using his influence to unite the two organizations in the Trade Union Confederation (CTC). This prevented the establishment of rival centres of power and enabled Castro to promote his priorities. This determination to secure full control was equally evident in his attitude to the political process.

His main goals were to promote employment, expand healthcare, extend education, and create a new political consciousness. In 1960 he told a million Cubans in Havana that the government would not hold elections, and the new regime rested on charismatic authority and the popularity of the reforms, rather than the institutional structures of Soviet-style communism. However, the relationships with the USA and the Soviet Union would play a key role in shaping the regime.

The US government was lukewarm about Castro from the start, and his visit to Washington in April 1959 did not allay its anxiety. The American administration might have responded positively to a request for aid, imposing conditions that would have bound the new government to the USA. Castro failed to ask, and the CIA and State Department began to plan his overthrow, with the rhetoric of confrontation escalating on both sides.

In February 1960, a high-level Soviet delegation visited Cuba and signed its first trade deal, followed by the establishment of full diplomatic relations. US sabotage then increased, culminating in an abortive attempt to overthrow the regime by supporting the so-called Bay of Pigs invasion by Cuban exiles in April 1961. The USA also initiated an economic embargo against the island. All this both strengthened popular enthusiasm for the revolution and fundamentally affected its nature.

In September 1960 Castro created the Committees for the Defence of the Revolution (CDR), and these units of volunteers played a key role in upholding the new system. But Castro also strengthened his alliances to ensure that US pressure could be resisted. The cementing of the relationship with Moscow soon led to the installation of nuclear missiles against the USA, almost leading to world war in October 1962.

From 1961 Cuba began to evolve towards a political system that resembled that of the Soviet bloc, with the pro-Soviet PSP becoming a more important partner in the governing coalition. Yet Castro waited until 1965 for the formal establishment of the Communist Party and the origins and early development of the revolution continued to lend it very specific characteristics. Cuba was never a Soviet satellite in the same way as the states in East-Central Europe—both history and geography were decisive in this respect.

Advances and setbacks

The social objectives of the new regime were immediately evident. In 1961 thousands of young volunteers were sent to rural areas to spread literacy and simultaneously to learn about agriculture. The hope was that this would break down the divisions between town and country. Hundreds of new schools were built, with teacher training massively increased. Healthcare was also taken to rural areas, with the building of rural clinics. However, there were economic difficulties, with a drop in sugar yields of over 30 per cent between 1959 and 1963. This soon led to more rapid socialization, and between 1964 and 1970 the whole of industry, commerce, and finance was nationalized and the state took over 70 per cent of agriculture. There were also wage increases for the poorest-paid workers and moves towards an equalization of earnings and consumption.

Conventional communists and Soviet advisers argued that, with a low level of development, workers needed higher wages and bonuses for increased productivity. Until the middle of the decade this view was influential, but Castro was close to Ernesto 'Che'

Guevara (1928–67), who was the most sophisticated theorist in the revolution. His emphasis was on exhorting the population to work through moral incentives. Castro endorsed Guevara's approach in 1966, culminating in the revolutionary offensive of 1968–70, with the whole economic strategy focused on harvesting and processing ten million tons of sugar in 1970. In the event, this target was not reached and production in other key sectors declined.

The episode also exposed resentments at increased work without material incentives, leading to foot-dragging, absenteeism, black-market activity, and other forms of quiet resistance. The sugar crisis led to a complete reorientation in policy, with more reference to Soviet experience, formalized in Cuban adherence to the Soviet economic bloc (Comecon) in 1972. In 1973 the CTC argued in favour of more material incentives and the government shifted in this direction and also increased the production of consumer goods. Reforms led to a less egalitarian pay structure and some market-related reforms, with greater decentralization and autonomy, with profit incentives for individual units in the state sector in both industry and agriculture. There was also more tolerance for limited private economic activity, although this was coupled with incentives to form farming cooperatives, which increased very rapidly. Many more goods were also made available without rationing, although basic necessities were still distributed in this way so as to protect the poor.

When the annual growth rate was almost 14 per cent between 1971 and 1975 the state made a major effort to increase female participation in the workforce, suggesting (as in Sweden) that economic pressures were important in initiating measures to bring about greater gender equality. The participation of women had increased only slightly from the Batista era—from 13 per cent in 1956 to 18 per cent in 1970. From 1974 gender equality measures were introduced and by the mid-1980s female participation had climbed to 37 per cent. This was the highest level of formal sector employment for women in the whole of Latin America and was consolidated by the increasing proportion of women in higher education, rising to over 55 per cent of all enrolments by 1986–7. The changes in the position of women also led to a decline in birth and fertility rates, with Cuba's pattern of family size far closer to the typical advanced industrial society than to its Latin American neighbours.

Great strides were also made in inter-ethnic relations. Before 1959 there was very substantial discrimination against the Afro-Cuban population, originally brought to the island as slaves. The revolution dismantled institutional racism and the 1976 constitution explicitly banned discrimination on grounds of race or skin colour. In many spheres of life there were vast improvements. In particular, equal access to education led to far greater upward social mobility, although there was still an over-representation of Afro-Cubans in lower-paid jobs.

The social changes strengthened support for the regime in both rural and urban areas and, despite an economic downturn in 1976, the average annual growth rate between 1981 and 1983 was 7 per cent at a time when it was negative in Latin America as a whole. Taken as a whole, the years between 1970 and 1985 were the most successful for the new regime economically, socially, and politically.

The social achievements of the Cuban regime were impressive in reducing poverty and moving towards equality. The medical advances were particularly remarkable, with Cuba soon having the most doctors, nurses, and hospital beds per capita in Latin America—an achievement even more remarkable as about 50 per cent of the country's doctors went into exile soon after the revolution. A special feature of Cuban medical development was its attempt to equalize provision between the towns and the countryside. Cuba thus became the only Latin American nation with a universal system of free healthcare across the country, and the diversity of provision was also exceptional. This was reflected in life expectation, which improved from being the third highest in the region (at 59) before the revolution to the top position (at 76) in 1992. There was similar progress in infant mortality rates, so that in 1990 the death rate for children in Havana was about half that for Washington, DC. Moreover, the quality and quantity of healthcare in the USA was far more discriminatory in terms of both class and race. The achievements in education were equally remarkable, with free primary, secondary, technical, and higher education for all, and a literacy rate of 96.4 per cent by the 1990s.

Yet there were also some underlying problems. First, during the 1980s a drop in the sugar price and a sharp reduction in a Soviet subsidy led to a debt of nearly $5 billion in 1986. This meant increasing dependency on Comecon, which accounted for 86 per cent of Cuba's total trade. Second, the government had also been seeking greater Western trade, tourism, and foreign investment. This brought in foreign currency, but also stimulated discontent by exposing the population to new inequalities. Third, the regime's strategy was sometimes unclear and contradictory, and there was an increase in prices, a drop of living standards, and a slight fall in wages. At the same time, some officials took advantage of their privileged access to foreign exchange for personal gain and built up informal power networks. In 1989 this led to the public execution of four very senior officials, with others imprisoned or dismissed from office.

None of these problems suggested that the regime faced a major crisis and it continued to rest on strong popular support. But there were vulnerabilities, and a cataclysm several thousand miles away now led to a crisis.

Crisis: the collapse of the Soviet bloc

The collapse of communism in East Central Europe in 1989 and the subsequent disintegration of the Soviet Union were crippling blows. By 1993 GDP had fallen by 34.8 per cent, with even more serious declines in several key sectors. The USA clearly believed that additional pressure would bring about the end of the regime, and in 1992 passed the Cuba Democracy Act (reinforced in a further Act in 1996), which tightened the embargo and specified that only the total removal of the Communist Party from power would be acceptable.

In effect, Cuba became a siege economy, designated 'the special period'. Power was shut off every day in each neighbourhood, there were shortages of necessities, and queues for rationed food. Because people had to spend so much time dealing with the basic requirements of life, there was an inevitable decline in productivity, and factories could not operate because they lacked raw materials or spare parts. The state maintained free medicine and education, but doctors needed to spend much of their time searching for equipment or drugs, and schools were also short of basic requirements. University admissions were reduced and a greater emphasis was placed on more practical education.

The government was aware that neither the economy nor the social system could survive on this basis, and it pursued a more aggressive attempt to attract foreign investment, with elements of privatization. Above all, it sought to turn Cuba into a major tourist centre. This brought some economic benefits, but also had some highly negative effects.

Almost immediately after the attainment of power in 1959, Castro had ended the sleazy nightclub culture that the island had built up during its dependency on the USA. Some of this now returned. The influx of tourists also had marked economic effects, and in 1994 a formal two-tier currency system was introduced, with the Cuban Convertible Peso pegged to the dollar, while state workers were paid in the Cuban Peso. This had little value and poorer people were reliant on the rationing system. Similar two-tier systems grew up elsewhere. Foreign tourists gained privileges of various kinds (including fuel allocations), while many Cubans were still struggling with acute shortages. Likewise, those who worked in the tourist industry received bonuses and tips, while those outside it had few such opportunities.

Increasing pressure from Washington reinforced the difficulties, while Castro's periodic reliance on overt repression strengthened the hand of the Cuban lobby in Florida in ensuring that no concessions were made. In this context, the imprisonment of seventy-five dissidents and the execution of three people for hijacking a ship and trying to sail it to Florida in April 2003 suggested that the regime was fighting for survival rather than progressively moving towards the professed goals of the revolution.

Yet the regime's endurance was remarkable. There was soon an increase in biotech and medical exports, the discovery of oil in the Gulf of Mexico provided a new lifeline, ties with several Latin American countries were strengthened, and the EU edged towards the resumption of normal diplomatic relations. However, the strategic direction of the regime was unclear.

Renewal?

In general, Fidel Castro was unwilling to go far in diluting the socialism of the earlier years and he sought to maintain the system with external economic help, particularly from the left-wing regime of Hugo Chávez in Venezuela and from China. However, there were strains, both in sustaining the economy and in securing sufficient popular enthusiasm and political support.

The succession of his brother, Raúl (b. 1931), began on a temporary basis in 2006, as Fidel became increasingly ill. Two years later Raúl assumed full state powers, also securing the leadership of the party in 2011. He announced economic reforms from 2008 onwards, soon demonstrating that these would be fundamental, rather than incremental. The rationale for a plan to update the economy, approved by the Party Congress in 2011, was to address the problem of low productivity.

The goal was to enlarge the private sector while providing employment opportunities for several thousand workers who would be laid off from state enterprises. Between 2010 and 2015, the private sector more than doubled and the non-state sector as a whole constituted nearly 30 per cent of the workforce. In 2016 Raúl presented a further document to the Party Congress, setting out the theoretical bases and essential characteristics of the new Cuban Economic and Social Model. This gave assurances of a continuing commitment to provide healthcare, education, social security, employment, housing, and some state subsidies. But it acknowledged that the economic reforms would lead to greater inequality with differential incomes for the various kinds of work. It also envisaged phasing out a million jobs in the state sector and reducing state subsidies, including gradually ending ration cards.

In purely economic terms it is easy to appreciate why Raúl Castro believed that major changes were necessary. By 2011, the production of goods was still below the pre-1989 level and state salaries were so low that many worked in the informal economy or emigrated, which became fully legal in 2013. But even on the government's statistics—widely regarded as excessively optimistic—there was little sign that the reforms were achieving Castro's goals, and by 2018 officials acknowledged that the rate of growth was less than half of what was needed.

Earlier there had been hopes that external support would provide some substitute for the Soviet Union, and the rapid improvement in relations with the USA during the last two years of the Obama presidency had seemed promising. However, by 2019 the rightward shift in Brazil and Colombia, the collapse of Venezuela, and President Trump's reversal of Obama's policies made Cuba appear increasingly isolated.

In social terms, the growth of inequality became a major problem, with the most obvious manifestation the growing gulf between the beneficiaries of tourism, with access to hard currency tips, and those dependent on the state. By 2017 a self-employed hairdresser or hotel waiter could thus earn at least twenty times as much as a state-employed neurosurgeon. Since the reduction of inequality was so fundamental to the revolution, this regression was very significant.

It also had a negative impact on ethnic equality because all aspects of the changes tended to disadvantage Afro-Cubans. They were less likely to live in areas where tourists sought accommodation, to have relatives abroad who could send money for start-up businesses, or have access to privileged medical treatment or private tutors for their children.

While the rise in inequality caused resentment amongst the disadvantaged, there was also dissatisfaction from educated younger people, who sought higher incomes in Cuba or new opportunities abroad. In fact, the substantial generational division between those steeped in the goals and values of the revolution and the more individualistic 'millennials' was a major problem. All this made it far more difficult to create the solidarity of the earlier period. This was indicated by the virtual disintegration of the CDR and a decline of 18 per cent in Communist Party membership between 2011 and 2016. And although there were now more channels, including social media, for the expression of diverse opinions, there was still harassment, intimidation, and arbitrary detention of human rights and political activists.

Yet the system continued to demonstrate extraordinary resilience. Between 2000 and 2017, Cuba consistently improved in many indicators of social progress, including life expectancy, maternal mortality, and key indicators of gender equality. Overall, the Human Development Index continued to place the country in the high category (at 73 out of 189 countries in 2018). And there was still far greater racial equality than elsewhere in the region. For example, a report by the Economic Commission for Latin America and the Caribbean in 2016 showed that 38.3 per cent of Afro-Cubans went on to post-school or tertiary education compared with 40.6 per cent for the rest of the population.

But it was also clear that there were major challenges in maintaining and renewing the system. In addition to the economic difficulties and changing international context, the fundamental question was whether a way could be found to secure adequate social and political cohesion for the next period.

This was not a new problem, for there had been periodic crises of legitimacy—for example, in the aftermath of the failure of the 1970 sugar campaign and in the 'special period' after the collapse of the Soviet bloc. However, the problems were particularly acute by 2019. First, in both material interests and world outlooks the population was more diverse than ever before. Secondly, the era of charismatic revolutionary authority personified in the Castro brothers finally came to an end.

In April 2018 Raúl Castro stood down as president, and was replaced by Miguel Díaz-Canel, who had been vice-president for the previous five years and was born after the revolution. Castro, now in his late eighties, remained first secretary of the party, but constitutional reforms indicated an intention to establish a more collective form of leadership in the future. In July of the same year a draft for a new constitution, open to amendment, was circulated to the public.

This maintained the leading role of the Communist Party, but several hundred changes were made in response to the consultation. Some amendments demonstrated the power of traditionalists, while others arose from younger people demanding a stronger commitment to the private sector and more open artistic expression. The final version agreed in December was submitted to a referendum in February 2019, where it was supported by over 90 per cent on a turnout that also exceeded 90 per cent of registered voters. The constitution sought to navigate between the different sectors of opinion. In response to the more traditional wing, Cuba's ultimate political goal was described as advancing towards communism, and the social conservatism of the older generation also led to the elimination of an explicit commitment to same-sex marriage. However, the earlier version had prohibited the accumulation of private property, which provoked opposition from the self-employed, and the final text compromised by allowing the state to regulate ownership on a case-by-case basis.

It is too early to predict the new leadership's attempt to steer a path between the different sectors of society and the diverse types of dissatisfaction that exist. But although there is little reliable evidence of public opinion, in 2019 it still seemed unlikely that the majority wanted a wholesale change of regime. Cuban socialism might yet be able to adapt and survive.

Sweden, Cuba, and socialism

Both Sweden and Cuba achieved much in relation to the socialist goals of equality, cooperation, and social solidarity. Clearly, their systems differed very markedly and the two countries were also at very different stages of development. Yet there were also some similarities. First, in both cases the social achievements remained dependent on sustainable economic success and became far more difficult to uphold when growth faltered. Furthermore, as time went on, it also became clear that the domestic economies could not be isolated from international economic pressures. Second, while egalitarianism was normally welcomed by poorer sections of the community, in neither state was it universally popular.

In Sweden the egalitarianism of the solidarity wages system and high taxation led to a backlash in the 1970s and 1980s and, more recently, large corporations and higher income groups have continued to push the system towards a more typical form of European capitalism. In Cuba there have been recurrent disputes over income differentials since the sugar crisis in 1970 and these now provide a major challenge for the regime. All this suggests that equality goals can never be taken for granted. Third, both the Swedish and Cuban models have passed their peak.

There are also important contrasts between the Cuban and Swedish experiences. Castro's revolution transformed Cuban society to a far greater extent than any impact made by social democracy on Sweden, where the system of private ownership remained in a concentrated form, and the changes necessitated compromises with political opponents and support by civil society organizations. In contrast, while the transformation in Cuba certainly elicited popular support, it was constructed from above through state- and party-dominated institutions. This difference has relevance for any prognosis about the two states.

In Sweden it seems reasonable to assume the continuation of liberal democracy for the foreseeable future even though we cannot be sure about its evolution—in particular, whether it will move further to the right or whether it will eventually move back towards a reinvigorated version of the earlier social model. In the Cuban case, we cannot have even this level of confidence about the future. US administrations have normally taken it for granted that most of the population will withdraw their support for the regime if there is continuing external pressure and Donald Trump has recently tightened sanctions. However, many would argue that an evolutionary process is more likely than any abrupt change of system.

It is also instructive to consider the experiences of Sweden and Cuba in the wider context of the recent history of social democracy and communism, which I will discuss in Chapter 4. The Swedish model has been trimmed, but is still recognizable, while social

Socialism

democracy in general currently appears to be in a state of crisis across most of Europe.

The experience of Cuba in comparison with the fate of other communist regimes is still more telling, for elsewhere they are generally of historical rather than contemporary interest. After the rapid collapse of the Soviet bloc between 1989 and 1991, communism as an international movement disappeared, even though states that described themselves as such remained, above all in China.

For much of the 20th century, and particularly between 1945 and 1990, communism and social democracy were the two dominant traditions of socialism, but, as discussed in Chapter 4, new forms of socialism have now appeared. However, before this, it is necessary to examine the challenge to the two dominant traditions that emerged from the mid-1950s onwards with the so-called 'New Left'. For the legacy of such movements also shapes our current era.

Chapter 3
New Lefts—enrichment and fragmentation

The rise of the so-called 'New Left' called into question the doctrinal and organizational forms of both communism and social democracy, and ushered in an era of direct action. This was epitomized in the student-led 'events' in Paris in May 1968, but similar eruptions occurred in many other parts of the world. The New Left was never a coherent movement, and included a wide range of ideas and tendencies outside the dominant traditions. A shared assumption of both communists and social democrats had been the primacy of the organized working class, which was now called into question in both theory and practice. This was accompanied by a rediscovery of older traditions, including more 'humanistic' interpretations of Marxism that had been submerged under the weight of Soviet orthodoxy, and a multiplicity of new intellectual influences.

1956 is often taken as the pivotal date in the emergence of the New Left. In the case of communism, the reasons are quite evident. In February Nikita Khrushchev, the Soviet leader, denounced Stalin at the Party Congress and then orchestrated an invasion of Hungary in November with other satellite states in order to ensure its continued adherence to the bloc. These two events led to an unprecedented exodus of communist party members, particularly in Western Europe, and many of them would seek new alignments. In the case of social democracy, there was no similar cataclysm because there was no equivalent centre, and each national party followed its own trajectory. In fact, the real crisis for social democracy arose later with the stalled growth and the increasing impact of economic internationalization from the 1970s, and this will be discussed in Chapter 4. However, the crisis of communism was also bound to affect social democracy, for Moscow had been the centre of Marxist thought since 1917 and the Cold War had reinforced this tendency.

Dissident ex-communists now encouraged a renewed interest in Marxism from those on the left who had never supported the Soviet Union. Others who rejected social democracy as too timid were drawn to new forms of extra-parliamentary politics that challenged existing theories and practices across a whole range of activity. Marxist thinkers, who rejected the orthodox emphasis on economics, also became influential in the New Left. In particular, a group of theorists, collectively known as the 'Frankfurt School' (from the Institute for Social Research based in Frankfurt from 1918 to 1933), which had always emphasized the importance of consciousness rather than class as the source of social transformation, was rediscovered.

Herbert Marcuse (1898–1979) became particularly important. In *Eros and Civilisation* (1955) he drew on Marx and Freud to argue in favour of both social and sexual liberation, while in *One Dimensional Man* (1964) he argued that the working class had become entirely integrated into advanced industrial society. Revolutionary transformation would now depend on 'outsiders', including ethnic minorities and radical intellectuals. Although his work was often obscure, its 'message' was in harmony with the movements of 1968. Battling against existing power structures and sexual conventions, students could cite Marcuse to legitimize their aspirations to create a new world.

Another earlier figure whose work became widely appreciated was Antonio Gramsci (1891–1937), the Italian communist leader who had been imprisoned by Mussolini from 1926 until his death. In his prison writings, he dealt extensively with the extent to which capitalist domination (hegemony), particularly in Western Europe, rested on ideas and assumptions as well as overt aspects of power. He stressed the need for socialists to create a new 'common sense', a 'counter-hegemonic project', based on alternative ideas, assumptions, and cultural constructs. This emphasis, which had some similarities with that of such thinkers as Stuart Hall (1932–2014) and Raymond Williams (1921–88), led many on the New Left to broaden the definition of the 'political' by including the realm of culture. They also now paid more attention to aspects of Marx generally ignored by both the Second and Third Internationals. His concept of 'alienation', which brought together the realms of consciousness and economic exploitation, appeared particularly relevant in the era of revolt in 1968.

Yet the New Left was not always deeply theoretical or even specifically socialist. For example, it supported the Campaign for Nuclear Disarmament, which was the biggest mass movement in Britain in the late 1950s and early 1960s. Moral outrage, rather than any conventional socialist notions, fuelled this protest. More generally, there were also diverse direct action movements in the later 1960s and 1970s, including squatters' movements, tenants' cooperatives, and women's groups. Some of these included people with a coherent socialist doctrine, some based themselves on anarchist ideas, but there were also numerous activists drawn to radical politics on particular issues without regarding themselves as socialist. International developments were also a key factor in the protests. The biggest single issue was opposition to the American-led war against the North Vietnamese, which generated major campaigns and demonstrations in many parts of the world. But when, in August 1968, the Soviet Union and some of its allies invaded Czechoslovakia to crush an attempt to establish a more pluralist form of communism there, the gulf between much of the New Left and pro-Soviet communists widened.

On the other hand, some of the socialist protesters were not really 'New Left'. For many other groups that claimed revolutionary Marxist credentials now challenged communist parties. In particular, there were numerous smaller parties, which argued that the Soviet Union had betrayed the revolution, while insisting that a vanguard party following the 'correct' line could still establish socialism. Many of these were inspired by Trotsky, who had argued that the rot had set in once Stalin abandoned the goal of permanent revolution and attempted to introduce socialism in a single country. Others looked to Mao, emphasizing the revolutionary potential of the masses and the need for vigilance against Soviet 'revisionism'. These Trotskyist and Maoist parties added to the diversity, and played an active role in many of the campaigns and protests of the era.

By the 1970s, the New Left had generated new social movements, which maintained that the dominant forms of socialist theory and practice were inadequate and they argued that socialism could be *enriched* by broadening its range. Defenders of orthodoxy, however, feared that the whole socialist project would be undermined by excessive concentration on these matters, leading to *fragmentation*. No doubt both were right, and certainly it now became increasingly difficult to define the doctrine. The old certainties disintegrated: socialism had become decentred.

By the 1990s the world had changed in many ways and younger protesters tended to regard the 1960s as a distant era. But new forms of direct action were developing. One key focus was in relation to 'globalization'. The term was now widely used and defined in various ways, but it was mainly associated with the removal of trade barriers, the loosening of domestic regulations, and the opening of all economies to international competitive pressures. Its advocates claimed that open markets would benefit everybody. But the key bodies that promoted this new orthodoxy were the G7 group of the major economies, the World Bank, the World Trade Organization (WTO), and the International

Monetary Fund. In reality, the impact of this form of globalization was highly unequal, both within states and globally. Amongst the advanced capitalist countries, the stark rise in inequality in the USA was particularly acute, and it was there that a major episode in a new global justice movement took place.

The protests came to a head when approximately 40,000 people converged in a mass protest in Seattle in late 1999, shutting down the meeting at the World Trade Organization. The media sought to discredit the movement by focusing attention on a violent minority, and this was repeated in the coverage of subsequent protests of this kind. However, the majority were demonstrating peacefully against the nature of contemporary capitalism or a particular aspect of it. Like the earlier New Left, this later generation of direct action was largely outside the control of the main political parties and tended to reject formal organization. But it was far more transnational. Taking advantage of the internet and social media, 21st-century activists have been fully aware of global developments. They have also been able to organize almost instantly to mobilize people for demonstrations or other forms of action and to secure international support.

In this respect the Seattle protests were emblematic of many subsequent eruptions of direct action. Thus in September 2011 a movement to 'Occupy Wall Street', the centre of the finance sector in New York City, had many international dimensions. The main focus of protest was against increasing inequality and the concentration of power and wealth at the top, with the key slogan 'We are the 99%'. The international dimensions of this action were obvious, for by October there were Occupy protests in at least 750 cities across the world.

Similarly, the Occupy movement in New York was itself influenced by international developments. 2011 was the year of the so-called 'Arab Spring' when mass action appeared to be dislodging a series of dictatorships in the Middle East. The protests in Tahrir Square in Cairo in January and February against the Egyptian leader Hosni Mubarak were sources of inspiration for the American actions. Very significant occupations against the current economic policies of the Spanish government in May were a further, and more comparable, international influence.

Like the earlier New Left, this kind of mass protest challenged existing assumptions, but there was a significant difference in the context. In the 1960s and 1970s, the guardians of orthodoxy had feared that direct action might lead to a decentring and fragmentation of socialism. But in the early decades of the 21st century many of the protesters no longer even viewed socialism as a key reference point. This chapter now focuses on two cases that spanned the whole period—the feminist and green movements.

Feminism

As equality, cooperation, and social solidarity are the core values of socialism, it *might* appear self-evident that it would regard the role and position of women in society as of critical importance. Yet socialists have not always been feminist and there has been a complex relationship between these two groups of ideas and movements.

There was a prolonged campaign for female suffrage during the 19th and early 20th centuries. This is often known as 'first wave feminism' and is distinguished from the so-called 'second wave', launched in the era of the New Left.

Some later feminists drew a sharp distinction between these 'waves', with the first allegedly confined to civil and political issues while the second embraced social, economic, and sexual issues. In fact, this is a simplistic distinction and it is equally unhelpful to insist that there is always a clear difference between socialist and non-socialist forms of feminism, for the boundaries between the two are fluid. Both earlier socialist ideas and wider feminist notions influenced New Left feminism, and this 'second wave' of the 1960s and 1970s in turn influenced later forms, which also covered a spectrum of viewpoints.

Some of the early socialists had made a real attempt to integrate male/female roles and relationships into their thought and practice. As part of his opposition to 'religious superstition', the 19th-century utopian socialist Robert Owen opposed Christian notions of marriage and regarded the traditional family unit as a barrier to cooperation. Owenites devised their own forms of sexual union based on ceremonies emphasizing equality and cooperation. In his bizarre way, Owen's contemporary, Charles Fourier, took sexual emancipation much further, regarding all forms of sexuality as legitimate and seeking to find outlets for them in his phalanxes. However, Marxist theory would have greater influence over subsequent socialist feminist ideas.

There were references to women in much of Marx's work, and he was conscious of the dual sources of their oppression in the economic and domestic spheres. Yet in general he tended to see the position of women as a *reflection* of the social and economic system. Capitalism made women subordinate, while social revolution would enable them to engage in creative labour. Yet there was no suggestion that they could be *agents* of this change although there was plenty of available material on which Marx could have based a less male-centred view of the working class. A further weakness in Marx's analysis was his categorization of work so as to include only the production of food and material objects, excluding such activities as child-rearing. By assuming the permanence of the division between production and the domestic realm associated with capitalism, he thus incorporated the contemporary hierarchy between men and women into the heart of his economic theory.

After Marx's death, Engels attempted to explain the position of women more fully in *The Origin of the Family, Private Property and the State* (1884). He took sexual relationships as of primordial importance in male/female roles, arguing that in early times women were dominant. They maintained this position after the establishment of the family because reproduction was necessary for the survival of the tribe and women produced the primary material goods—bedding, clothing, cooking utensils, and so on. All this changed, he claimed, as the domestication and breeding of animals, controlled by men, became increasingly important economically. As men became dominant in the production process and created the system of private property, the power relationship between the sexes shifted. Men now wanted to pass on their property to their own children and subjugated women within the household. According to Engels, it followed that the emancipation of women depended upon the abolition of private property.

As many later feminists would note, there were unexplained assumptions in Engels's interpretation. Why should women have controlled such resources as bedding, clothing, and cooking unless there was already a sexual division of labour *before* the development of private property? And why should men have taken control of animal husbandry? And if such differences in the gender roles existed before the advent of private property, how did it follow that the ending of capitalism would necessarily emancipate women? Such questions had practical relevance after the Bolshevik revolution.

Almost immediately, the new Soviet state established full citizenship for women, and equality was rooted in economic independence and the right (and obligation) to work. Labour laws provided for equal pay and other protections, and a new family law addressed the household dominance of fathers, introduced civil marriage and divorce on demand, abolished illegitimacy, and legalized abortion. But there were also some early signs of tension.

Clara Zetkin (1857–1933) was a founder member of the German Communist Party, but in 1921 took charge of the Communist

International Women's Secretariat and spent most of the rest of her life in the Soviet Union. However, soon after the Bolshevik revolution, Lenin admonished her for encouraging women members of the Communist Party to discuss sexual matters, when the 'first state of proletarian dictatorship is battling with the counter-revolutionaries of the whole world'. Of greater historical significance was the fate of Alexandra Kollantai (1872–1952), the first Commissar of Social Welfare, who initiated some early Bolshevik reforms.

Kollontai went far beyond Engels in integrating economic and sociopsychological factors in her accounts of the position of women. In 1920 she headed a special department within the Communist Party (the *Zhenotdel*) devoted to women's issues. Until 1922, she organized nurseries, daycare centres, maternity hospitals, and restaurants so that women could be relieved of the double burden at work and at home. She also instructed workers in the *Zhenotdel* to inform people of their rights, protest against abusive male workers, and push for the inclusion of women at all levels of decision-making. She wrote about the socialist relationship between women and men, advocating complete abolition of existing family structures in favour of love based on attraction and a joint commitment to creating a new society. She also called for the communal upbringing of children and urged communists to revolutionize the family. However, her theories and policies were not well received by other Soviet communists. In 1922, she was dismissed from the *Zhenotdel*, which now channelled its activities into the more traditional 'caring' role, with an emphasis on the socialization of housework and childcare, provision of social services, food distribution, and nursing those who had been wounded during the civil war. In 1936 Stalin outlawed abortion and restricted divorce.

After the Second World War women in the Soviet bloc countries were far better represented than their counterparts in Western Europe (outside Scandinavia) in terms of higher educational

attainment and professional and political status, but little
attention was paid to the issues that Kollontai had raised in
relation to the household itself. For example, by 1989, 80.2 per cent
of children from birth to 3 were in crèches in communist East
Germany, and 95.1 per cent between the ages of 3 and 6 in
kindergartens, but the government assumed that women would
continue to play the main role at home. The objective was to
enable women 'to reconcile the demands of their job still more
successfully with their duties towards child and family'.

The record of social democracy in general was at least as
unsatisfactory. Second International socialists had often been
ambivalent about allying with campaigns for female suffrage,
instead emphasizing the need to emancipate working-class
women through employment outside the home. In reality, the
practices and underlying assumptions of the parties were often
highly conservative. During both world wars, women were
brought into the labour force in jobs previously reserved for men,
but were subsequently pushed back into more traditional roles,
with social democrats generally taking the same line on this as
other political parties. And while the development of welfare
states certainly benefited working-class women economically, the
systems assumed that the male would be the breadwinner while
the female would continue to occupy the domestic role. Nor did
most social democrats have much sympathy with those who
emphasized the personal and sexual aspects of the oppression of
women. In general, male-dominated labour movements tended to
view those who advanced such ideas as middle-class feminists,
whose preoccupations had no relevance for most women.

Yet after the Second World War, the position of women in
advanced capitalist societies changed very considerably. There was
a vast growth in female employment, educational opportunities
increased, and, with them, higher aspirations conflicted with
prevailing assumptions. Labour saving devices in the home
provided a little more time for other activities, and new forms of

contraception finally removed the fear of pregnancy from sex. Such changes culminated in 'second-wave feminism' in the late 1900s.

The movement for women's liberation in this period contained a whole range of political positions, but many socialist feminist thinkers now took issue with Engels's account of the position of women. In her influential early post-war text, *The Second Sex* (1949), Simone de Beauvoir (1908–86) argued that women had been regarded as 'the other' in a male-dominated world and there was no reason to assume that the abolition of private property would overcome this. She regarded socialism as a precondition for female emancipation, but many later feminists criticized her own position for accepting the male definition of the world rather than seeking to recast it. For she argued that women should transcend their 'otherness' by engaging fully in traditional masculine pursuits.

Juliet Mitchell (1940–) provided a more rigorous examination of Marxist theory in 'Women: The Longest Revolution' in *New Left Review* (1966). She suggested that the oppression of women arose from both ideology and from their position as workers in the capitalist system. This meant that socialism would not automatically resolve their position since there needed to be an ideological revolution as well as transformation in the system of production. Others argued that the Marxist account had no relevance at all, and a key text was *Sexual Politics* (1971) by Kate Millet (1934–2017). She argued that the relationship between the sexes was based on power and sustained by the ideology and social structure of 'patriarchy', irrespective of the economic structure. Socialists, particularly Marxists, resisted this kind of interpretation, but it is here that the experience of 1968 and its aftermath became so relevant.

The dominant ideology of the movement was one of participatory democracy and a resistance to traditional hierarchies and organizations. Yet, as Geoff Eley put it:

In 1968, girl friends and wives were present with their men. They made the coffee and prepared the food, wrote the minutes and kept the books. They handled the practical tasks, while decision-making, strategizing and taking the limelight stayed with the men. Flagrantly contradicting the anti-hierarchical and participatory ideals of the 1968 movements, this taken-for-granted status soon led to anger.

The result was the development in many advanced capitalist countries of active women's movements. These included campaigns for more traditional socialist concerns, including trade union rights, equal pay, and wider social, economic, political, and cultural equality. But feminists also adopted a new form of organization, often with small groups of women raising issues of concern and supporting one another in collective activities. A typical approach was of 'consciousness-raising', where women were encouraged to share their experiences, gain more confidence to express their views, and participate in collective decision-making. The best-known slogan encapsulating the approach was 'the personal is political'. This could have been Clara Zetkin's riposte to Lenin, for it was based on the contention that issues of sexuality, relationships, and experiences in the home were highly 'political'.

The typical structure was of networks rather than formal organization, as implied in the term 'movement'. There was a strong reaction against the hierarchy and bureaucracy associated with formal institutions, including parties and trade unions. Instead, the emphasis was on participation, learning from experience, and local activity. This was combined with some national and transnational campaigns on particular issues. For example, a movement to 'reclaim the night' to stop sexual violence developed from an International Tribunal of Crimes against Women in Brussels in 1976 and was followed by action in several countries.

Second wave and New Left feminist thought developed a whole range of interpretations of the sources of women's subordination, resulting in a broadening of socialist theory and notions of organization. However, by the 1980s the movement had passed its peak. There were various reasons for this, but the most significant was that Margaret Thatcher in the UK and Ronald Reagan in the USA initiated the era of 'neo-liberalism'. They countered the visions of liberation and emancipation, which had inspired 'second wave' feminism, with authority and 'traditional family values'. In place of the collective notions of solidarity and cooperation, neo-liberalism held that women could succeed through their individual aspirations and choices. Behind all this, the changes in the economic climate were of fundamental importance.

The 1960s were years of rapid economic growth in most advanced capitalist countries. 'Second wave' feminists generally assumed that this would continue, and that women could and should share fully in its benefits. Socialist feminists also stressed the need for redistribution so as to bring about equality. But after 1973 there was a slowdown in growth with rising unemployment. In this harsher economic climate, it became far more difficult to sustain the earlier sense of confidence and optimism about the full emancipation and empowerment of women.

There had always been divisions within the feminist movement, which now increased. For example, there were tensions as to whether men should be included or excluded; whether feminism should adhere to political parties or remain entirely separate; and whether all women should be part of a single movement or if differences of class and ethnicity necessitated the formation of distinct groups. Socialist feminists had maintained a strong sense that they were part of a wider left-wing movement with shared values and goals, but neo-liberalism simultaneously undermined the solidarity of both feminism and socialism.

Other challenges also arose, leading to 'third wave' feminism from the mid-1990s. A particular feature of this has been a profound questioning of assumptions that all women share a collective

identity with universal characteristics and needs. One aspect of
this was to criticize the extent to which New Left feminism
tended to prioritize the concerns of women in advanced
capitalist societies. In principle, socialist feminism was
committed to the global solidarity of women, but did the
feminism of the Global North genuinely accept the diversity of
notions of female emancipation? Or did it really adhere to a
'Western version'?

In 1984 Chandra Talpade Mohanty had already posed this
question in an influential article, 'Under Western Eyes: Feminist
Scholarship and Colonial Discourses'. This was a powerful critique
of the implicit notion that all women in developing countries were
similarly oppressed and that the West needed to 'rescue' them.
Mohanty demanded a genuine recognition of both the range of
women's experiences in different societies and the diverse means
through which they sought liberation and emancipation. This
argument remained pertinent in the 21st century as many women
who fled poverty and war in the Global South faced new barriers
in Europe, where the generally secular assumptions of Western
feminists often conflicted with many other cultural and religious
traditions.

The representation of women from particular minority groups
presented a rather similar challenge. In particular, many black
women in both the USA and the UK claimed that white feminist
movements failed to address the particular forms of discrimination
that they faced. Highlighting a triple form of oppression, on the
grounds of race, gender, and class, they sometimes formed entirely
separate groups. However, in a key article in 1989 Kimberle
Crenshaw approached such combined forms of discrimination in a
novel way by introducing a new concept, which would become
extremely influential—'intersectionality'.

Crenshaw argued that the existing laws of sexual and racial
discrimination in the USA failed to alleviate the problems of

low-income black women. The laws focused on a single axis of discrimination—either of race or sex—but, as she demonstrated, these dealt mainly with those who were the more privileged in one of these two categories. However, poor black women faced a compound form of oppression through the intersection of these dual dimensions. Crenshaw's most fundamental points were about the structures of society and the multiple sources of oppression.

Earlier, one of the major fears of many socialist feminists was that the development of separate identity groups would undermine the possibility of solidarity and collective actions. However, Crenshaw's concept of intersectionality did not advocate separation. Instead of adopting a 'top-down' approach to the ills of racism and sexism, it was, she maintained, necessary to begin 'with addressing the needs and problems of those who are most disadvantaged'. This was also the 'most effective way to resist efforts to compartmentalize experiences and undermine potential collective action'. In practice, the coalescence of intersectional interests and ideas could converge into collective action.

One example of this occurred when the inauguration of President Donald Trump in January 2017 provoked a worldwide 'Women's March'. Within the USA this was the largest single-day protest in history, and other marches took place across the globe, with estimates of the total numbers worldwide ranging from between 3.3 to 4.6 million (see Figure 6). The demonstrations brought together diverse groups. Some were mainly concerned about issues with the most obvious relevance for women, but others were motivated particularly by fears about racism, immigration controls, peace, and climate change. Intersectional interests fostered the creation of alliances and mutual influence between groups and individuals in a situation when they each perceived threats to their values and goals.

Many of the protesters' ideas about solidarity, equality, rights, and justice, and also their explanations of the causes of oppression,

6. The global dimensions of the women's marches in January 2017.

resembled those of the 1960s and 1970s. There have also been some attempts to combine the socialist feminism of the earlier generation with the new themes. Thus in 2019 three women launched *Feminism for the 99 per cent: A Manifesto*, which sought to overcome stale oppositions between 'identity' and 'class politics'. It aspired to unite 'existing and future movements into a broad-based global insurgency'. Yet the similarities and links between the earlier New Left and 'third wave' feminism should not be exaggerated. There were significant differences in ideology, theory, and general assumptions because of the changes in the general context between the two eras. Nevertheless, together both generations have brought about fundamental changes. Progress has not been linear or sufficient, but it would now be difficult to envisage viable socialist theories or organizational forms and practices so dominated by men and masculinity as in the first half of the 20th century.

Green socialism

From the 1970s onwards, the rise of green politics provided a further challenge to traditional socialism. The most obvious aspect was in the greater appreciation of the threats to the environment and ecological life, but, like feminism, green conceptions also put forward alternative political and economic models, favouring decentralized community organizations, small-scale technology, and non-hierarchical and non-bureaucratic forms of democracy.

Precursors of green approaches had long existed within socialism. Many of the utopian socialists wanted to recreate the rural communities that capitalist industrialization was undermining, and even Robert Owen was wedded to the idea of small-scale production. Probably only Saint-Simon was an enthusiastic supporter of industrialism per se. Similarly, the anarchists, Proudhon and Bakunin, opposed capitalism partly because they believed that it was destroying more 'natural' human associations based on cooperative relationships in the countryside.

Although most socialists in European societies subsequently became reconciled to industrial society, these earlier traditions continued to exist. For example, the guild socialist movement in early 20th-century Britain sought to combine the notion of medieval guilds of crafts with modern trade unionism. One of its thinkers, A. J. Penty (1875–1937), coined the term 'post-industrial society', calling for a drastic reduction of large-scale industry in favour of small-scale production within communes.

Of course, many non-socialists had also been concerned with such issues. Some critics of the industrial revolution were deeply conservative and the modern environmental and ecological movement also crossed conventional political boundaries. *Silent Spring* (1962) by Rachel Carson (1907–64) certainly had a radical edge. This was a scathing critique of the devastating impact of synthetic pesticides, which inspired a grassroots movement in the USA and also influenced environmental and ecological protests, including left-wing activists, across the world. However, other influential works had little specific relationship with socialism.

This was the case when, in 1972, the Club of Rome, which included current and former heads of state, UN bureaucrats, high-level politicians, government officials, scientists, economists, and business people, produced *The Limits to Growth* (1972). This would eventually sell thirty million copies, making it the best-selling environmental work of all time. It argued that resource depletion was inevitable on the current trajectory of growth and that humanity must take effective action to prevent 'overshoot and collapse'. The same year saw the publication of another influential report, 'Blueprint for Survival', but the key author, Edward Goldsmith, was on the right of the political spectrum, and called for people to live in small, decentralized and largely de-industrialized societies.

The emergence of green approaches in the 1960s and early 1970s was therefore not solely from within the left, but the New Left soon became involved. One key reason was the reluctance of the dominant forms of socialism to abandon their long-held assumptions about industrial growth. During the economic downturn in the early 1970s, social democrats continued to see the solution as increased government expenditure to restore full employment. Nor would communism accept demands for fundamental changes, and manufacturing industry in the Soviet bloc was notoriously toxic. This disregard for the environmental aspects of industrial expansion was one of the major causes of the nuclear disaster at Chernobyl in the Ukraine in 1986. Given the priority that both social democracy and communism placed on industrial growth, they therefore either tended to ignore the growing evidence of environmental and ecological damage or to dismiss it as anti-socialist propaganda.

This combination of complacency and denial was one catalyst for many in the New Left increasingly to embrace the green challenge, but there were also additional reasons. Germany, where the most influential green movement developed, is an exemplar of this more general tendency. Opposition to the SPD for entering a Grand Coalition with the Conservatives (CDU) between 1966 and 1969; frustration with bureaucracy and hierarchical organizations; and involvement in the mass protests of 1968, were all contextual factors. But an important spark, bringing about the formation of the Greens in 1980, was a campaign against nuclear power.

Green movements and parties rapidly proliferated and, although they were not ideologically homogeneous, they stimulated an enhanced consciousness of the dangers of environmental and ecological degradation. At the same they provided a critique of the dominant models of economic and political organization, encapsulated in the word 'sustainability'.

From the late 1980s a new era began with increasing evidence of the urgency of the situation and the magnitude of the tasks in making the necessary transformations. The report in 1987 by the World Commission on Environment and Development (Brundtland Commission) was significant in its stress on the interrelationships between the varied ecological and environmental threats. This, and the pressures from green groups and activists, raised the international salience of these issues, bringing about a new emphasis on the need for green energy, the recycling of waste, and changing patterns of consumption. There were also campaigns for boycotts of environmentally damaging goods, such as pesticides and genetically modified food, and lobbying to end investment in fossil fuel industries.

But the transformative issue was the growing recognition of the devastating effects of climate change. There had been increasing scientific concerns about global warming since the 1970s, but an important turning point came with a World Meteorological Organization Conference in Toronto in 1988 and the establishment of the Intergovernmental Panel on Climate Change (IPCC). The Rio Earth Summit in 1992 then established the United Nations Framework on Climate Change (UNFCC) as the main international agreement on climate action. In 1997 the Kyoto Protocol set the first legally binding emission reduction targets for developed countries. But, despite later attempts to reinforce the Protocol and a Paris Accord in 2015 to limit global warming 'well below' two degrees Celsius, the climate crisis constantly grew more perilous.

By 2020, both the scientific evidence and experience of exceptional weather patterns across the world, including storms, flooding, and excessive heat, had combined to make climate change the most important issue of the age. In late 2018, the IPCC thus warned that temperatures were on track to reach 1.5°C above those in the pre-industrial period between 2030 and 2052 and to double this level by the end of the century. Once the temperature reached two degrees of warming there would be a massive reduction in animal and plant life, many low-lying coastal regions and island territories would become uninhabitable, and millions would be driven from their homes. Climate change also contributed to violent conflict, migration flows from the Global South to the Global North, and threatened to exacerbate poverty and inequality.

These dangers have brought about a quantitative and qualitative change in the green challenge to socialism (and all other political doctrines) and also an increase in direct action protests on the issues. There have been such protests across the globe against international companies for causing devastating effects on traditional ways of life and livelihood—from the Inuit in the Arctic, to the Ogoni in the Niger delta, to small island communities in widely dispersed locations. Furthermore, an important strand in the mass action in Seattle in 1999 focused on multiple environmental and ecological threats, and the 'climate justice' movement, born at that time, has been increasingly active during the 21st century.

As with contemporary feminism, the movement has been transnational and particularly attractive to younger people (see Figure 7). Additional momentum was injected in 2018 when Greta Thunberg was able to launch a global movement for school

7. Young people protesting about climate change in 2019.

strikes, injecting a sense of urgency about the issues to politicians and governments across the world.

However, the protest networks are also often intergenerational, as, for example, in spring and autumn 2019, when the Extinction Rebellion network closed the streets and bridges of central London.

In reality, the dichotomy on climate change between activists and more conventional political actors, such as social democratic parties, may be less stark than it sometimes appears. Thus many activists accept that ultimately only governments, including those at regional and local levels, can implement the necessary measures to attain climate change targets. For this reason Greta Thunberg devoted considerable efforts to addressing decision-makers across the world, most notably through a fifteen-day yacht journey across the Atlantic to the annual UN climate talks. At the same time, many of those who worked primarily in and through institutions no doubt welcomed external pressures through direct action to boost their own efforts.

However, there are often very significant differences between activists and conventional political actors about the extent of the changes required. In some respects, this is a continuation of the debates in the earlier period when the dominant forms of socialism resisted green demands for a radical transformation. In general, social democratic parties and governments, which accept the compelling scientific evidence about the vast human responsibility for climate change, have remained far more cautious than many activists have demanded. For they normally favour a mixture of taxation and pricing systems, laws and regulations, and targets for bringing about change rather than any dramatic transformation.

Nevertheless, there were certainly advances during the 21st century. In the earlier phase of the green challenge, many believed that social democracy faced intractable problems in making the necessary changes because limiting industrial expansion would undermine the basis for its employment and welfare policies. In contrast, Michael Jacobs (1960–), who has produced many theoretical works on the green economy and was also a policy adviser for the British Labour government from 2007 to 2010, has suggested that social democracy is particularly well placed to deal with the current environmental challenges. Arguing that a form of class collaboration was necessary to establish the post-war welfare state following the crisis of capitalism in the 1930s, he has suggested that a similar form of cooperation could now simultaneously address austerity and ensure that contemporary social democracy incorporated green imperatives into its economic policies. More generally, social democracy now took the problems increasingly seriously. For example, by 2019 European social democracy in general (in the transnational Party of European Socialists) accorded far greater weight to the need for a green transformation than previously, although the aspirations were more ambitious than the concrete commitments.

Yet by the time climate change was recognized as such a critical question, the political context had changed. As discussed in

Chapter 4, socialist and social democratic parties faced increasing problems in the first two decades of the 21st century, and often they formed alliances or coalitions including green parties and movements. There were also signs of a partial fusion in thought—often known as a 'red–green' alliance. Even in the UK, where the electoral system constrained the growth of green parties, there were theoretical developments of this kind. Thus in 2008, economists and environmentalists from different parts of the Left launched the 'Green New Deal' to counteract the impact of both the financial crisis and climate change. In 2015, Ann Pettifor, one the group's members, joined the Labour Party's Economic Advisory Committee, and in September 2019 launched a new version, demonstrating the necessity for a new system of finance to transform the economy from its dependence on fossil fuels.

Perhaps more notably in international political terms, in February 2019 Alexandria Ocasio-Cortez, the newly elected Congressional Representative for a district in New York City, pioneered a 'US Green New Deal' in 2019. She was also a member of the Democratic Socialists of America and the fourteen-page summary of the plan, which she jointly proposed with Senator Edward Markey, linked climate change goals to wider socialist goals (see Box 2).

While the general context has changed since the first developments in the green challenge in the 1970s, this has, of course, been the most marked in relation to communism. In the first phase, when the Soviet bloc was so resistant to accepting limits to ecological arguments, some argued that the fundamental problem was that Marx had assumed unlimited industrial production. In particular, Rudolf Bahro (1935–97), who was a committed communist in East Germany and later an important figure in green politics in West Germany, made a powerful and influential critique of Marxism, insisting that the deeply negative side effects of industrialism in the Soviet bloc were inherent in the theory itself. But, by the time climate change was generally recognized as the overwhelming

Box 2 The US Green New Deal

Key Features

o It builds on October 2018 Special Report on Global Warming
by ICC Panel and President Roosevelt's New Deal in the
1930s to combat the Great Depression

o It recognizes US historic responsibility for its
disproportionate amount of greenhouse gas emissions and
therefore the duty to take a leading role in reducing
emissions through economic transformation

o A ten-year Green New Deal mobilization includes:

• Building resiliency against climate-change-related disasters

• Upgrading infrastructure

• Meeting 100 per cent of the domestic power demand with
clean, renewable, and zero-emission energy sources

• Building up or upgrading energy-efficient 'smart'
power grids

• Spurring massive growth in clean manufacturing and
industry

• Working with farmers to cut pollution and greenhouse gas
emissions

• Overhauling transportation, with electric vehicles, clean,
affordable public transportation, and high-speed rail

• Removing greenhouse gases, including by bolstering forests

• Making the US the international leader on climate action and
helping other countries to achieve a Green New Deal

o Goals and projects to realize the goals and mobilization
include:

(continued)

Box 2 Continued

- Providing and leveraging adequate capital (including through community grants, public funds, and other public financing)

- Ensuring democratic and participatory processes inclusive of and led by frontline and vulnerable communities at the local level

- Ensuring high-quality union jobs at family-sustaining wages and benefits

- Strengthening and protecting union rights

- Obtaining free, prior, and informed consent of indigenous people for all decisions affecting them and their traditional territories

- Providing universal high-quality healthcare, affordable, safe, and adequate housing, economic security, and access to clean water and air, healthy affordable food, and nature

threat, the Soviet bloc had long since collapsed and there was no coordinated communist response.

Certainly, there has been a very dramatic change in China, which had previously industrialized at breakneck speed, creating massive environmental hazards. Subsequently, it became a world leader in many forms of innovative green technology and also made enormous progress in improving air quality and reducing other forms of pollution. However, in 2018 increased fossil fuel consumption within China led to an increase in greenhouse gas emissions for the second successive year, and 25 per cent of coal plants under development elsewhere in the world depend on Chinese funding. The new domestic measures have been impressive, but have been introduced through the highly repressive regime and China remains the world's highest global gas emitter.

However, there have been significant theoretical discussions within Marxist circles, with many refutations of the earlier arguments of Bahro. In particular, Kohei Saito came to the opposite conclusion in an important book in 2017. After a thorough analysis of Marx's unpublished and published works, this concluded that his enthusiasm for industrial production was short-lived while his ecological convictions were deep-rooted. In Saito's view, Marx's vision of socialism clearly 'includes a project to rehabilitate the social and natural metabolism that has been seriously distorted in capitalism'.

Finally, climate change activists also often incorporate elements of socialism into their critiques and demands. When the climate justice movement was established in 1999, a major focus was on the role of the corporate industrial and financial sectors in generating the problems. Similarly, in an influential work, Naomi Klein blamed unregulated capitalism, and its primary beneficiaries and advocates, for the catastrophic ecological damage that they were causing across the world. In general, the loosely organized climate justice movement, like the contemporaneous 'third wave feminism', has not used the traditional language or concepts of socialism. Yet it has been anti-capitalist, sharing many socialist goals and values, including the key priorities of ending poverty, privilege, and inequality. A popular slogan in the international youth protests in 2019 was 'system change, not climate change', and there is a widespread conviction that corporate capitalism is the major driver of climate change.

Socialism has always been concerned with human society as a whole, rather than with compartmentalized questions about economic and political organization. With both natural and social scientists now emphasizing the range of the threats posed by climate change, socialism clearly needs to develop an adequate response to these fundamental questions. By the end of the second decade of the 21st century, it may not have succeeded in this task, but considerable efforts are being devoted to it and, like their predecessors in the New Left, activists again played a crucial part in raising consciousness about the dimensions of the challenges.

'Beyond the fragments'?

In the era of the New Left, feminists and greens (and several other movements) challenged the dominant forms of socialism. For traditionalists, such developments were alarming, for fragmentation could threaten to undermine socialism both as a coherent world outlook and in its organizational forms. However, the pressures that produced these new ideas and movements suggested inadequacies in the existing ideological and organizational structures. A text from 1979 that sought to combine feminism and socialism was very illuminating in its attempt to define a new approach.

Beyond the Fragments (1979), by three socialist feminists, Sheila Rowbotham, Lynne Segal, and Hilary Wainwright, soon became an influential work, both in the UK and internationally (see Figure 8). It confronted the fact that socialism was no longer unified in doctrinal or organizational terms, but contained several movements and ideas. While acknowledging that this was leading to fragmentation, the authors also regarded the new ideas and movements as positive and they believed that a more pluralist form of socialism could now be created.

The most substantial essay was by Rowbotham, the socialist historian. Her preoccupation at the time was to strive against centralized party structures, typified by Soviet-style communist parties, but also by many of the contemporary revolutionary Marxist sects and parties in the New Left. Several of her insights were equally relevant for contemporary social democracy and trade unionism. She called for organizations with forms of internal association that would actively overcome discrimination through the open expression of difference between the particular

BEYOND THE FRAGMENTS
Feminism and the Making of Socialism

Sheila Rowbotham, Lynne Segal
and Hilary Wainwright

8. Beyond the Fragments.

groups. But she was equally anxious that the goal of socialism should not be replaced by a whole set of entirely distinct social movements based on the notion of separate identities and exclusively concerned with their own economic, cultural, or ethnic oppression. All the subordinated groups needed to work together in recognition 'of creativity in diversity and a persistent quest for open types of relationships to one another and to ideas as part of the process of making socialism'.

This was both a thoughtful analysis and an arresting vision of a possible future. But it was also a product of a particular era. When *Beyond the Fragments* was republished in 2013, Rowbotham reflected on the differences between the two eras, but also on continuities and possible lessons from both. She recognized the positive aspects in the later generation of protest and protesters, particularly the global dimensions and the greater consciousness of the environment and climate change. But she also noted that, as the possibilities for radical change had receded with the economic changes after the 1970s, the assertion of fixed identities became more pronounced. Her generation had aspired to create a rejuvenated form of socialism, but the fragmentation was now so extreme that opposition to the iniquities of contemporary capitalism could no longer 'cohere into any single name'.

Her most significant insights came from her comparative historical analysis of both eras. In the 1960s it had seemed urgent to contest assumptions that Marxism was a fixed dogma and to view it instead as a valuable source to be mulled over. But it was now difficult for younger generations to enter the political and cultural framework of that era imaginatively because contemporary outlooks were so different. Younger generations, she suggested, should read varieties of Marxist theory as well as the history of anarchism, gay liberation, and movements against colonialism and racism. History provided no models, but it was wise to be conscious of the snags and insights in all past radical traditions when considering the tasks for the future.

There was widespread distress in response to the devastation caused by contemporary capitalism, but dissenters seemed to be 'left to grumble in isolated clusters'. Perhaps the coalescence of these forms of opposition into some form of unity would result in a reformed capitalism, but the New Left had sought something more—transformation and liberation into a world characterized by association, trust, and cooperation. It was necessary to reclaim this sense of hope: 'an inestimably powerful starting point if we are to go beyond being just anti-capitalism to conceiving what else might be'.

This powerful exhortation drew on past traditions of socialism marginalized in the years of communist and social democratic supremacy, but also in the climate of selfish individualism and competition that replaced them. In Chapter 5, I will consider the continuing relevance of this kind of vision. But first it is necessary to consider the impact of the collapse of communism and the erosion of social democracy, and some recent attempts to implement alternative forms of socialism in practice.

Chapter 4
Beyond the dominant orthodoxies

The end of an era

By 2020 almost thirty years had elapsed since the collapse of the Soviet Union brought an end to the period in which two forms of socialism had been so dominant. The ending of Soviet communism was obviously not responsible for everything that subsequently occurred, but the momentous events unleashed by the downfall of the Soviet satellite regimes in 1989 had a transformative effect on the world in general and socialism in particular.

The final stages came very quickly. When Mikhail Gorbachev (b. 1931) became the Soviet leader in 1985, a total change of system seemed unlikely, but his desperate attempts to implement reforms brought about the collapse. His decision to let the East-Central European regimes go their own way was of critical importance (see Figure 9). The communist systems in these states had always been dependent upon Soviet power and they crumbled quickly. The escalating political, economic, and national crises within the Soviet Union then led to Gorbachev's resignation in December 1991, and the end of a historical era. The impact on socialism as a whole was not immediately obvious, but became fully apparent in the decades that followed.

9. German citizens help each other climb the Berlin Wall on 10 November 1989. The dismantling of the wall symbolized the collapse of communism in the Soviet bloc.

The Soviet system had always differed from many of the principles, values, and goals of socialism, as defined in this book. Even after the death of Stalin and the extreme horrors of his rule, the Soviet regime had remained a bureaucratic and oppressive dictatorship in many respects. Immediately after its disappearance some therefore believed that this might even strengthen the appeal of socialism by removing its negative associations. There was also a hope that there might now be both a unification of Europe and a synthesis between communism and social democracy.

But this was not to be. The enlargement of the EU, with the entry of many of the East-Central European countries between 2004 and 2013, brought about a partial unification of the continent, but this was not by fusing the two traditions that had separated in 1919. And, more generally, it was unrealistic to believe that the end of the Cold War might strengthen socialism, for this failed to appreciate the global ramifications of the Soviet collapse.

The very existence of the USSR had been a pressure to restrain capitalism within the more industrially advanced capitalist states, enhancing their commitment to public services and social provision after the Second World War. Competition between the Soviet bloc and the West had also meant that a state-led model of development was established in many poor countries in the Global South, and various left-wing regimes across the world could count on some Soviet support. As discussed in Chapter 2, this was crucial for some of the major social achievements in Cuba, which began to wane after the end of the Cold War.

The removal of the Soviet bloc also led to a very dramatic shift in international relations and international political economy. During the last decade of the 20th century, the USA was able to carve out its 'new world order' without any other power providing serious resistance. This enabled it to pursue an open-market strategy far more aggressively and there was a surge towards a global liberal economic system that imposed great pressures on governments that sought alternative approaches.

To suggest that the collapse of the Soviet bloc had such an immense effect raises an obvious question: could China, the most populous country in the world, now replace the Soviet Union as a pole of attraction for a communist form of socialism? Its economy was expanding at an unprecedented rate and by 2020 it was a competitor to the USA economically, militarily, and in terms of political influence. In theory, Chinese leadership of a new communist bloc was possible and, as Julia Lovell has argued, Maoism (interpreted variously) has continued to exert influence across the world and remains a major force with the potential to inspire revolutionary movements. Yet there are good reasons for doubting whether China could play the same role for *socialism* that the Soviet Union once did.

First, China does not offer an entirely different social and economic model from that of capitalism. After the death of Mao Zedong in 1976, the new rulers introduced extensive economic reforms, which established a form of capitalism in a one-party state. After 1993 it went still further in encouraging a business culture, embracing the pursuit of private wealth. It became extraordinarily successful in terms of growth rates and international competitiveness, but this led to a sharp rise in inequality between social classes, regions, and rural and urban populations.

Second, the regime has resorted to extreme repression. When the Soviet bloc in East-Central Europe was collapsing in 1989, the Chinese leadership sought to prevent any similar disintegration by brutally mowing down protesters in Tiananmen Square, and human rights were never recognized. Autocratic control became still more pronounced under Xi Jinping, who assumed the leadership at the end of 2012. His 'iron fist' was epitomized in the treatment of the Uighurs and other Muslim populations incarcerated in compulsory 're-education' centres. More generally, China is one of the most controlled systems in the world, with unparalleled levels of surveillance and state policing of access to information. Under Xi Jinping the private sector grew, but with increased party control and enhanced state penetration.

The rise of China has been highly impressive and the speed of change from an impoverished and largely peasant-populated state to that of a modern superpower is remarkable. In its most recent period of development, it has introduced some significant environmental reforms, and there has also been considerable progress in the provision of social services. Thus China has much to teach the world, but not as a new model for socialism. Nor does it even offer a clearly defined alternative approach to economic development. It has offered aid and investment to many countries in the Global South without attaching the same kind of political strings as the West. This may be helpful to the countries in question, but the strategy is designed to enhance Chinese power rather than to advance socialism.

Without dominant poles of attraction for socialism, the specific characteristics of the new era differed in each region and country. The following discussion of Europe and Latin America highlights both contrasts and points of comparison between two very different regions.

Europe

Europe was the birthplace of socialism and the site of major achievements, but there were major setbacks in the 21st century. Much of this section highlights these, but it is important not to exaggerate the reversals. First, despite a rise of inequality, Europe remains the most equal region in the world. Second, while social and health support mechanisms have been restructured, making life far more difficult for much of the population, and particularly for the most disadvantaged communities, social and public services remained at a higher level than in most parts of the world, including the United States. Thirdly, in relation to the recent past in Europe, there were many gains as well as reversals. In particular, EU enlargement meant that ordinary people could now move freely and live, work, and study elsewhere. In principle, the whole area was now also committed to democracy and human rights. These were largely gains in liberalism, but, as this book has stressed, such freedoms are also aspects of socialism.

Yet the rapid change brought major problems, for the collapse of the communist bloc caused fundamental difficulties, some of which only became apparent several years later. The most obvious impact was in East-Central Europe where, between 1989 and 1991, a swathe of countries changed very quickly from a communist model of socialism to a capitalist system. The economic change was not solely responsible for all the transformations in the area, for there were also latent ethnic, national, and religious conflicts that had been simmering for decades or even centuries. But the change of system was certainly a catalyst for other forms of upheaval. A horrific war in Yugoslavia (continuing until 1999) led to the break-up of the country and the birth of seven successor states; Latvia, Lithuania, and Estonia secured independence from the Soviet Union; Czechoslovakia divided into two states (in 1993); the former East Germany adhered to both the EU and NATO as a result of German unification; and between 1999 and 2017 twelve other former communist states joined NATO. This rapid transmutation was destabilizing and, as would become increasingly evident during the second decade of the current century, right-wing extremism and hostility to both socialist and liberal values became marked in several of the post-communist states.

The collapse of the Soviet Union also soon eliminated communism as a significant political force in Western Europe. In many countries, and particularly in Italy and France, there had been powerful communist parties after the Second World War.

These had played important roles in opposing the most serious negative features of the right, but they now generally disintegrated, quickly losing support. In some countries, ex-communists merged with other left-wing socialists or with green parties. Such parties and groups often played valuable roles in highlighting issues of concern for socialism, but generally only as minority political forces.

Yet the most significant change in West European socialism after 1991 was the erosion of the former dominance of social democracy, particularly in the northern and north-western part of the continent. Even before the downfall of the Soviet bloc, the shift from a broadly Keynesian economic system to a more neo-liberal one had led to a malaise in social democracy, with the parties struggling to define their own economic and social policies. The pressures to introduce market systems into the public sector, coupled with the ideological assault on notions of working-class solidarity, caused them great difficulties. As in the Swedish case, there was also a fundamental change in the nature of the labour movement and workforce, both of which had been so important in underpinning social democracy.

There were always differences between individual countries, but in all the advanced capitalist economies there was a decline in manufacturing industry and a rise in the service sector, with an increase in part-time and temporary work. This was coupled with a shift away from the living and working conditions historically associated with the labour movement. The general trend was towards more atomized employment and the dispersal of traditional working-class communities.

The globalization and liberalization of the international economic system intensified the pressures. These included the triumphant political mood in non-socialist circles about the total supremacy of capitalism. In 1990 the sociologist Ralf Dahrendorf (1929–2009) thus proclaimed:

> [T]he point has to be made that socialism is dead, and that none of
> its variants can be revived . . .

Social democracy, he argued, had made itself redundant by
tempering the excesses of unconstrained capitalism. More
generally, he concluded that the historical law of Marxism had
been inverted, for it was capitalism that succeeded socialism. In
this context, all forms of European socialism were now on the
defensive.

However, social democracy added to its own problems through
major weaknesses in policy. In general, it failed to provide a
critique of the new dominant model of capitalism or to mount
effective opposition to it. The approach was generally to endorse it
while aspiring to mitigate its most negative effects. The Labour
prime minister Tony Blair, who assumed office in 1997, with
Gordon Brown as chancellor of the exchequer, was pre-eminent in
this trend. Achieving power with a rather vacuous slogan of
offering a 'third way' between capitalism and socialism, the party
(with Brown taking over the leadership in 2007) won three
elections before losing power in a general election in 2010.

For much of this period, the Labour government provided some
significant social benefits through increased public expenditure,
which funded improvements in such areas as health, education,
and infrastructure. However, it accepted the existing economic
model, and did not address damaging underlying trends. These
included the continuing break-up of traditional working-class
communities, a reinforcement of regional inequalities, and an
enhanced share of national wealth and income for the very richest
sectors of society. At first there was some reluctance amongst
other European social democratic parties to embrace the Labour
government's approach in its entirety, but they generally moved in
the same direction, with broadly similar effects on their societies.
Although many parties continued to be relatively successful in
electoral terms in the 1990s, this masked a long-term decline in

their support, which became more pronounced in the early years of the 21st century. The share of the vote for social democratic parties thus declined by approximately 20 per cent between the mid-20th century and 2010.

The world financial crash of 2007–8 exacerbated all the problems of social democracy. The general policy prescription of neo-liberalism when governments suffered from a sharp decline in revenue was to implement cuts in expenditure and changes in welfare and social provisions in order to reduce budget deficits. International financial institutions and right-wing economists and political parties were largely responsible for devising these 'austerity' measures in response to the financial crisis. But the most severe impact fell upon poorer sections of societies, which tended to be traditional supporters of social democratic parties.

Between 2008 and 2013 there was a general rise in electoral volatility and increased political fragmentation, which continued and intensified throughout the second decade of the century. But social democratic parties suffered the most severely from this phenomenon. This was particularly the case with those parties in office for parts of the crisis period, including the Panhellenic Socialist Movement (PASOK) in Greece, the SPD in Germany, the Spanish Socialist Workers Party (PSOE), and the Dutch and British Labour parties. Yet even when social democratic parties were not in office or primarily responsible for the harshest measures, austerity undermined their support by reducing or restructuring the provision of social services and public sector employment.

All this aggravated the final key problem facing social democracy, for it cultivated conditions conducive to a climate that was hostile to both socialism and liberalism. The gulf between those benefiting from the economic system and those suffering from its effects thus played a major role in the rise of xenophobic, 'nativist', racist, and populist right-wing parties (subsequently collectively termed 'the radical right'). These had been growing in significance since the mid-1990s in much of Western Europe, but increased migration provided them with new opportunities to make inflammatory and sensational claims. Myths about migrants from East-Central Europe taking jobs and housing, undercutting wages, and fraudulently securing social security benefits developed in the aftermath of EU enlargement. This kind of mobilization then gained still more traction with the rapidly rising numbers of people seeking to enter Europe so as to escape poverty and violent conflict in the Global South during 2015–16. As already noted, several states in East-Central Europe also embraced xenophobic ideas, sometimes in still more extreme forms.

All this brought together a set of factors which threatened social democracy and socialism more generally: neo-liberalism undermined working-class communities and increased the gap between the beneficiaries and victims of globalization; austerity policies exacerbated all these tendencies; and the radical right mobilized support by claiming that 'outsiders' and a metropolitan elite were responsible for the problems. But there was one additional component in this toxic mix: its negative impact on support for the EU.

European integration had primarily been the creation of the political centre—above all, social democracy and Christian democracy. These two blocs of opinion had driven the project forward since 1958 and, in all the direct elections to the European Parliament from 1979 to 2014, had secured a majority. Some sections of the left had long criticized integration for creating a capitalist bloc, and this view gained some support once the EU reinforced the pressures towards neo-liberalism and austerity in the 21st century. In contrast, social democracy and many other forms of European socialism generally supported European integration as a contribution to peace, international cooperation, and social, environmental, and human rights. However, the radical right used the failure of the EU to deal effectively with migration to reinforce the message that 'Europe' was responsible for the problems that people were encountering in their daily lives and, once again, this posed particular difficulties for social democracy.

In the UK the effect of this combination of pressures was evident when the UK Independence Party (UKIP) and sections of the Conservative Party mobilized support for 'Brexit', which secured a narrow victory in the referendum in June 2016 (51.9 per cent to 48.1 per cent on a turnout of 72.2 per cent) with majorities for 'leave' in many more Labour Party constituencies than 'remain'. Under similar pressures, national elections in several other EU countries in 2017 and 2018 showed a collapse of the social democratic vote, perhaps most notably in France, where support for the Parti socialiste declined by 32 per cent, with an overall loss of 286 seats.

In the 2019 European Parliament elections, perhaps against expectations, parties and movements generally in support of the EU emerged with greater strength than its outright opponents, partly because green parties and other sectors of the left also made gains. But there was no outright majority and, on the left of the political spectrum, there were differences both between and within countries. European socialism in general, and social democracy in particular, was thus facing many difficulties and uncertainties.

Yet even during these challenging years, there were some significant opportunities and positive developments. Both the periodic eruptions of social protest and social survey evidence showing continued support for values associated with welfare states suggested a potential for galvanizing socialist or 'socialistic' parties and movements. Furthermore, feminist, green, and other social movements had reshaped socialist ideas and movements, providing a broad basis of potential support for alternatives to the current form of capitalism. The fragmentation of the earlier orthodoxies also facilitated the emergence of various combinations of broadly left-wing parties that continued to promote particular parts of a socialist agenda. There were occasions when it seemed that such opportunities might be exploited successfully, although none achieved a breakthrough. In this context, three quite different attempts have some significance.

The first was with the creation of a new party, Podemos ('we can'), in January 2014. This needs to be understood in relation to the events of 2011. The impact of the financial crash in Spain was particularly severe. GDP fell by approximately 15 per cent between 2008 and 2013, with the rate of unemployment growing from 8.2 per cent in 2007 to 26 per cent overall in 2013, reaching 55.5 per cent for those under 25. On 15 May 2011, demonstrations and occupations against austerity policies introduced by the PSOE government took place throughout the country. The socialists' inadequate response to the financial crisis led to the return of the right-wing Partido Popular (PP) to government in the general elections in November and its retention of office until 2018. But the May protests also led to the *los indignados* (outraged) movement, which persisted at a high level of intensity for several months and at a lower level for much longer (see Figure 10).

Almost three years later Podemos was established to turn the mass protests into an entirely new social movement and party, influenced by the developments in Latin America.

Podemos achieved an extremely rapid rise to prominence, and in 2015 achieved 20.66 per cent of the vote and over 5,212,711 votes—only just behind the PSOE. But this was also the peak of its popular success. Many of the reasons for its failure to advance further were outside its control, but it was only in its very early stages that it appeared to be an entirely new kind of party, based on adamant opposition to free market globalization and the promotion of alternative policies. Of equal significance, it was in

10. **Mass protests by the Indignados Movement (also referred to as 15-M) in Spain in 2011.**

this initial phase that it also promised to transcend traditional notions of party hierarchy and organizational structure and build connections across diverse communities in society.

It never successfully reconciled the contradictions between building from the 'bottom-up' in a decentralized movement, and the ambitions of a group around its leader, Pablo Iglesias (b. 1978), to become a national and governmental party. In order to achieve this, they watered down the party's economic policy and subverted the system of decentralized democracy, leading to internal splits and disillusionment. It remained a significant party in conventional terms, but it never fulfilled its early promise as a new kind of party.

A second attempt to challenge neo-liberal austerity was in Greece, with the very rapid rise to prominence of the Coalition of the Radical Left (Syriza), which emerged from a series of splits and regroupings going back to the 1960s. This achieved an electoral victory in January 2015, bringing it to government under the leadership of Alexis Tsipras (b. 1974), with over 36 per cent of the popular vote. The success or failure of this administration would be defined by its ability to change the terms of austerity demands from the 'Troika' of the EU, the European Central Bank, and the IMF.

In 2010 Greece had faced bankruptcy because of its large budget deficit, but, in response to its appeal for help, the Troika imposed two Bailout Loan agreements, which caused enormous hardship and deprivation. By 2015 overall unemployment was 25.8 per cent (with youth unemployment at 49.6 per cent), and since 2008 output had declined by 26 per cent, with a fall in wages of 23.5 per cent. Syriza sought to 'Europeanize' the issue, but it generally failed to secure concrete support. Its attempts to persuade the Troika to change the terms of the bailout conditions for a loan were abortive, and Tsipras called a referendum on whether Greece should accept the demands. On 5 July 2015 the voters rejected the conditions by a very large majority, but Tsipras ignored the result, leading both the government and party to split. After winning a further election in September, Syriza subsequently implemented the austerity programme. Having imposed hardship for four years, it lost the next election in July 2019, enabling the right-wing party New Democracy to regain power.

Syriza had demonstrated the possibility of rallying popular support for opposition to the current capitalist orthodoxy, but the climb-down undermined the momentum to bring about change. Whether it was possible for a small country with a relatively weak economy successfully to challenge larger powers and institutions has remained a subject of debate, but the case of Portugal provides some evidence for the viability of an alternative approach. Having also experienced the devastating effects of an austerity package dictated by the 'Troika' between 2011 and 2014, in 2015 the Socialist Party (a social democratic party) was elected to government, with the support of the Communists and two other small left-wing parties. This reversed many of the social expenditure cuts, while growth recovered and the budget deficit was reduced to the lowest level in forty-five years.

The British Labour Party provides a third example of a potentially significant development. After losing power in 2010, a new leader, Ed Miliband, attempted to steer a middle course between Blair's approach and that of traditional Labour Party policies. However, after the party lost a general election, Jeremy Corbyn was unexpectedly elected to the party leadership in September 2015. He had long been a left-wing critic of previous policies, and the party now attracted a very large number of recruits, swelling its ranks from around 190,000 to a peak of approximately 564,000 in December 2017. But the new members were a diverse group. Some were long-term left-wing socialists, who had been in other movements outside the party, or had deserted it because of the Blair–Brown policies. Others, particularly younger people, were motivated by a belief that Corbyn sought an entirely different kind of party, more akin to a social movement. Nor was there ever reconciliation between Corbyn and the majority of Labour MPs, who were completely opposed to him.

The party formulated more radical policies than in recent years, including those seeking to counter neo-liberalism and austerity and to implement a 'Green New Deal'. However, it failed to achieve power in the 2017 election, and the Brexit issue exposed major internal divisions. When Boris Johnson, the new right-wing Conservative leader, called an election in December 2019, using 'Brexit' as the main mobilizing issue, he achieved a parliamentary majority of eighty. Following Labour's fourth successive defeat, there was a leadership election to replace Corbyn in the early months of 2020. Yet many of the more radical policies of the past four years now appeared to be embedded in the party.

None of these attempts to challenge neo-liberal globalization was therefore successful. However, each contributed something of specific importance to European socialism. Podemos eventually disappointed many of its most enthusiastic early supporters, but it demonstrated the potential for a new kind of left-wing political party based on far greater decentralization and grassroots participation than the hierarchical and tightly controlled organizations associated with both social democracy and communism. Similarly, the wider impact of Syriza's struggle to combat the international demands for austerity measures demonstrated the resonance of the call to separate socialist notions of European internationalism from neo-liberalism. Unlike both Podemos and Syriza, the Labour Party is a long-established party that has formed governments for almost a century. Its current position is difficult and its future uncertain, but its rapid transformation and partial regeneration in 2015 calls into question any assumption of an inevitable decline in European social democracy or socialism.

Latin America

Despite some notable exceptions, for most of the period after the Second World War the prospects for socialism in Latin America appeared rather bleak. Of course, this is a vast continent with enormous diversity between and within the countries, so any generalization is oversimplified. However, there were extreme levels of poverty and inequality in most Latin American societies, which were also marked by the legacy of colonialism. In the late 20th century there were still many right-wing dictatorships often following neo-liberal economic policies, which exacerbated all the existing forms of injustice. The history of attempts to introduce socialism was also discouraging, because of both domestic repression and US intervention.

Yet at the turn of the 21st century, there was a major change. Beginning with the victory of Hugo Chávez in the presidential election in Venezuela in 1998, there was a significant shift to the left elsewhere in the continent—Brazil in 2002, Argentina in 2003, Uruguay in 2004, Bolivia, Chile, and Ecuador in 2006,

Paraguay two years later, and Peru in 2011. There were very significant differences between the various governments in this so-called 'Pink Tide', but the general shift to the left was highly significant, and many saw Latin America as a new standard bearer for socialism in the Global South.

The peak of success was early in the century when there was an increase in growth rates in the regional economy in contrast with trends elsewhere. To some extent the 'Pink Tide' was dependent on favourable trade and balance of payments conditions in international markets. The fact that the USA was preoccupied elsewhere and China was playing a new economic role in the region was also helpful for the left. The economic expansion continued until 2012, but by 2015 there was a marked downturn and in that year it also became clear that the left was in decline.

In general, Pink Tide governments brought about a significant change from the previous era, with far more inclusive social policies, attempts to address the most extreme forms of inequality and poverty, and some transformative gender policies. In 2014 there were female presidents in Chile, Argentina, and Brazil, and many countries implemented progressive laws on same-sex marriage and gender equality. However, the economic downturn led to greater internal conflict and instability, and from 2015 there was a decisive shift to the right in much of the region. This was reinforced after Donald Trump became president in January 2017, when the USA actively sought to reassert its control in Latin America. But even where there had been particularly decisive setbacks, it seemed unlikely that all the gains would be reversed. In Argentina, for example, Cristina Kirchner, who was vilified and discredited in 2015, returned to power as the pivotal figure (though formally as vice president) in the election in October 2019.

The most radical breaks from capitalism during the left-wing era were attempted in Ecuador, Venezuela, and Bolivia, where new regimes embarked on projects to bring about fundamental transformations. They retained the notion of class conflict in relation to the exploitation of workers and peasants, but also paid particular attention to the communities that had faced additional forms of marginalization and discrimination in the colonial and post-colonial regimes. The exclusion of indigenous peoples was of central importance in Ecuador and Bolivia.

Inevitably, the fact that all three governments sought, and partly implemented, radical changes meant that there was also serious domestic conflict, with attempts at sabotage by right-wing opposition. In Ecuador increasingly sharp division and tension led to the fall of the Rafael Correa government in 2017, but the other two countries offered partially contrasting cases. I will deal with Venezuela briefly, while discussing Bolivia more fully.

Socialism in Venezuela was not solely the creation of Hugo Chávez, but it was inseparable from him. He had previously been a professional soldier and it was in the military that he moved to the left, establishing a revolutionary movement in 1982. His first attempts to take power were through two unsuccessful coup attempts in 1992, but he eventually accepted the growing evidence that an electoral strategy could be successful. In 1998 he became president after securing over 56 per cent of the popular vote.

Throughout his time in power there was increasing polarization, both internally and domestically, about the fundamental nature of the 'Chavista' regime. For its supporters it constituted a new form of democracy for the mass of the people. They emphasized its continuing popularity, confirmed in each election, and its social and economic reforms. In contrast, both domestic opponents and the USA vehemently denounced the new regime, focusing on its appointments of reliable supporters to all the higher echelons, frequent constitutional changes to consolidate power, creation of a personality cult, and suppression of liberal democracy.

Within four years, these conflicts came to a head with a coup attempt in which the US government, under President George W. Bush, played a covert role. The supporters of Chávez immediately secured his return to power, but all this intensified both domestic antagonisms and the enmity between the two countries, with the USA demonizing Chávez and encouraging opposition to him. The Venezuelan leader mobilized popular support by constantly denouncing American imperialism. From then until his death in 2013, the conflict never abated.

The main success of the regime lay in its social achievements through extensive programmes and initiatives to combat inequality and poverty, particularly after the crises in 2002. Thus between early 2003 and the end of 2008, poverty fell from 54 per cent of households to 26 per cent, with extreme poverty reduced by 72 per cent. When the benefits of social programmes are included, the changes are still more dramatic: for example, infant mortality fell by more than one-third from 1998 to 2007, while higher education enrolment rates doubled from 1999–2000 to 2007–8. There was also a substantial reduction in inequality. Like Cuba until the 1980s, Venezuela seemed to be a success story in social policy, in both regional and international comparisons. And Chávez, like Castro, achieved considerable political solidarity, particularly through communal organizations. However, the source of funding for these achievements was deeply problematic.

Holding the largest reserves in the world, the Venezuelan economy and export industry had long been dependent on oil. In 1976 the mainly foreign-owned industry was nationalized, with the creation of Petroleos de Venezuela (PDVSA), but the company was structured as a business with minimal government regulation and most of the profits sent abroad. Under Chávez there were immediate conflicts over control, and in December 2002 the PDVSA executives refused to cooperate with the government, and called a strike, bringing about a major crisis for the regime shortly after the failed coup attempt. Chávez eventually withstood all the economic and political pressures and consolidated his control. In 2006 and 2007, he fully nationalized oil exploration and production by seizing the assets of US major oil companies and subsequently the government enhanced its ascendancy through further nationalizations.

The way in which Chávez now pursued his policy was flawed and unsustainable. Despite much talk about diversifying the economy, this did not take place and by 2009 oil accounted for 96 per cent of Venezuela's exports—a higher level than in 1998. The regime also relied on oil revenues to fund the social reforms, and provided excessively subsidized oil prices to consumers.

Apart from the numerous social and political benefits in diversification, this over-dependence on a single sector was extremely dangerous from an economic point of view, for a fall in world prices for oil would be catastrophic—and this happened under his successor, Nicolás Maduro. The government then claimed that the economic problems resulted from US sanctions after 2014 and other forms of sabotage, but, while these and the burden of debt repayment reinforced the problems, its own strategy was ultimately responsible.

Even when international oil prices were at their highest level in July 2008, governmental revenue dropped because oil production began to fall, and by 2013 general economic growth was declining. By 2016 it was minus 10.1 per cent and Venezuela experienced a 40 per cent fall in both necessary imports and profits from oil export. All this led to a free fall in the economy, hyperinflation, a humanitarian crisis, the reversal of the social gains, and near civil war in 2019. In this situation the USA orchestrated an abortive coup attempt, which failed largely because Maduro maintained the support of the military. But by June of that year the UN estimated that more than four million refugees and migrants had left the country.

The catastrophe was ultimately attributable to the attempt to create the permanent mobilization of disadvantaged people without an adequate economic policy or political institutions in which political power was genuinely dispersed with robust forms of accountability, control, and democratic participation.

The attempt to bring about a social and political transformation in Bolivia had some similarities, but also many striking differences. When Evo Morales became president at the beginning of 2006, Bolivia was the poorest country in the region. It was also characterized by extremes of poverty and inequality, with the minority 'white' and Mestizo population (of mixed Spanish and indigenous heritage) controlling the overwhelming majority of power at the expense of indigenous peoples. The economy depended on mining and, more recently, also on natural gas industries, which were under foreign ownership. Furthermore, there was enormous disparity between the regions, with wealth centred in the Santa Cruz region in the east of the country.

Attempting to create a socialist society would mean confronting international economic power, overcoming, or at least neutralizing, the hostility of the business sector and affluent middle classes, and simultaneously seeking emancipation and equality for those disadvantaged by both class and identity. These would be formidable tasks, but, paradoxically, the injustices of the recent past also worked to the advantage of the new regime.

In 2000 President Sánchez Lozada had taken the decision to privatize a public and communal water source in Cochabamba, situated in a valley in the Andes, and to sell it to a US multinational corporation. This made water unaffordable for the local Quechua population and led to mass protests for three months, finally bringing about the abandonment of the project. Three years later Lozada attempted to privatize gas and open it to foreign participation, again precipitating mass direct action, primarily by indigenous groups. The government resorted to extreme violence, but this repression undermined its support. Lozada fell and was followed by two short-lived presidencies before the election that brought Morales to power. He thus took control when there was already a momentum for a new government to seek fundamental change, with support for a shift in the ownership of key resources.

In the late 20th century, significant alliances between rural peasant communities and former miners had developed. The catalyst was the closure of many mines and the migration of former unionized workers to the countryside. This led to new organizations, which reflected reciprocal influences between indigenous communities and those from an urban working-class background. In 1998 the Movement for Socialism (MAS) was created, which brought Morales to power in the election at the end of 2005.

MAS disavowed any suggestion that it was a conventional party, regarding itself as the instrument of social and community movements, and it also distrusted the state and political institutions, convinced that change came through pressures from below. Morales had been a social movement activist and eventually the leader of a union of coca leaf growers in a mountainous part of central Bolivia, just north of Cochabamba. The union, which included both former mineworkers and traditional coca growers, also provided social services for the community and was highly participatory, with decisions taken by consensus.

Building on the momentum for change, on 1 May 2006 Morales ordered the military to occupy energy fields. He put the oil and gas reserves under state control and ordered foreign producers to channel future sales of hydrocarbons through the state-owned energy company, subsequently renegotiating contracts so as to provide the state with a bigger share of the profits. This, and further nationalizations, meant that the Morales government became dependent on exports from extractive industries. In 2016, the petroleum industry still accounted for approximately 33 per cent of government revenues, 80 per cent of exports, and 18 per cent of GDP, and from 2006, the government also developed and sold natural gas. This dependency resembled the situation in Venezuela, but Morales avoided the excesses of Chávez.

The first two years of the MAS government were dominated by major battles with the former power holders, including over the nationalization policy, but the new regime remained extremely popular and both Morales and MAS won landslide victories in the 2009 elections. In the same year, a highly participatory constitutional assembly drew up a new constitution, which was ratified in a referendum. This simultaneously highlighted a commitment to shifting power towards the previously excluded indigenous communities and bringing about social and economic equality (see Figure 11).

The interrelationship between these goals was demonstrated in a World Bank report in 1994 showing that 73.5 per cent of the indigenous population was living below the poverty line, with 37 per cent in extreme poverty, and the gap between the indigenous and non-indigenous populations continued to widen before Morales came to power.

The new constitution also included a change in the name of the country with great symbolic importance—from the Republic of Bolivia to the Plurinational State of Bolivia—and significant concrete steps were taken to translate this into reality. There were guarantees to respect traditional cultures, allowing indigenous peoples to operate according to their own political, judicial, and economic systems, and a new ministry was established to promote internal decolonization. There were also very significant educational changes at all levels to bring about language equality and usage, and three indigenous universities were established (Aymara, Quechua, and Guarani). There was recognition of thirty-six cultures, each with their own language, but they did not all acquire the same benefits, partly because they varied considerably in size.

CONSTITUTION OF THE PLURINATIONAL STATE OF BOLIVIA

Enacted on February 7th, 2009 by
President Evo Morales Ayma

Translated to English by
Luis Francisco Valle V.

11. The constitution establishing Bolivia as a plurinational state in 2009 had importance in symbolizing change.

Morales's government made progress towards the wider social and economic goals in the MAS programme. There was a rapid rise in minimum incomes from 2005 and by 2014 extreme poverty had declined from 37.7 per cent to 17.3 per cent and from 63.9 per cent to 36.1 per cent in rural areas. Equally important were the direct social benefits to various groups. For example, pregnant women received benefits on condition that they attended medical check-ups and later brought their children to clinics for examination. Some criticized the coercive aspect of such measures, but they contributed to a reduction in mortality rates. Similarly, the state encouraged school and university attendance through the availability of free provision.

Both the indigenous policies and the more general social reforms also had an impact on the representation of previously disadvantaged peoples in social and political institutions. The share of middle-class professionals in the national legislature declined from almost 50 per cent in the 1990s to less than 20 per cent by 2014, while the share of workers, artisans, and those employed in the primary sector grew from just under 4 per cent to more than 26 per cent, and, at 30 per cent, the representation of women also reached its highest ever level.

All these changes showed the benefits of the new regime, but there were also tensions. Social movements, which were primarily rural, brought Morales to power, but both the transition to government and changes in society led to a shift. MAS became more urban and many new members reflected the growing middle-class and professional population. Their elevation to higher levels simultaneously weakened both the ideological commitment of MAS, and the working-class and indigenous representation in the circles around Morales. There was also a fracturing of the movement, with some key members remaining close to him while others were alienated and sometimes took up oppositional positions. The political institutions and civil service remained quite weak, with Morales becoming increasingly dominant.

The capture of overwhelming power in the 2009 elections also strengthened the executive, which was not checked by any strong party or parliamentary control. The opposition fragmented, but Morales continued to mobilize popular support in the same way as before. A further significant stage in this process came in 2011 with a judicial reform bringing in the direct election of judges, which also strengthened the role of the executive.

Morales maintained popular support, which was again confirmed in the elections of 2014, but the dynamics of the situation changed. He consulted the social groups within MAS less frequently, and his erstwhile allies, rather than the right, now sometimes resorted to mass protests to block his policies. Tensions also developed as a result of contradictory pressures: delivering the MAS programme, accommodating the economic demands of the extractive industries, and satisfying the growing middle-class and urban populations.

In 2011 Morales seemed to be bending to industrialist pressures when he suddenly announced a decree ending subsides on fuel, which caused a price rise of up to 82 per cent, quickly leading to direct action and strikes by unions. Almost immediately, he backed down and revoked the decree, but this episode indicated some of the problems in reconciling social goals and economic policies. There were also conflicts over the government's land reform and redistribution programme.

There was significant progress in the early years, with important gender dimensions. Previously women had normally been excluded from land ownership, but by 2013 25 per cent of land titles had been granted to women, with another 37 per cent issued to men and women jointly. But the pace of registering and redistributing land slowed down after 2011 and there were conflicts between different sectors of the original MAS coalition over land reform—particularly between settlers in the outskirts of protected areas in eastern lowlands and indigenous groups, which regarded such territories as their ancestral lands. In addition, there were problems in reconciling the goals of land redistribution with the need for increased food production.

There were still greater contradictions in other major policy areas. As an expression of the commitment both to indigenous people and the environment, the constitution included the principles of respect for Pachamama ('Mother Earth') and *vivir bien* ('living well'). In international forums, Bolivia gave radical critiques of international climate change commitments, achieving a positive reputation in many climate justice circles. It thus hosted 'The World's People's Congress on Climate Change and the Rights of Mother Earth' in Cochabamba in 2010, attracting 30,000 people from across the world.

In practice, though, the environmental record of the Morales government was mixed, and the most obvious clash between the earlier commitments and governmental priorities began in August 2011 with a proposal to build a major road from La Paz through the Isiboro Sécure National Park and Indigenous Territory (TIPNIS). The government claimed that this was to provide better access for local economic development, but TIPNIS was in the ancestral home of three indigenous peoples (with a total population of less than 12,500). The central segment of the road would bisect the reserve, which was protected, both as an indigenous territory and a national park, with the local peoples collectively owning most of the land and subsisting through fishing, hunting, and foraging in one of the most biodiverse regions in the world.

When a group of the indigenous peoples organized a protest march to La Paz, police violently harassed them, and the government also encouraged a counter protest by settlers in surrounding areas, who believed that improved transport links would enhance local economic development. Other social movements supported the protesters and, amidst bitter allegations on both sides, Morales appeared to back down in 2011. Yet six years later he again authorized the construction of the road, and protests and counter-protests continued. While the government divided and sought to discredit the opposition, its fragmentation also reflected wider complexities in the evolution of Bolivian political, economic, and social life, as well as the inherent difficulties in translating constitutional commitments into practice.

One final contradiction between theory and policy concerned gender. The constitution specified gender parity between parliamentary candidates and after the 2014 elections 53 per cent of seats in the national parliament were held by women, including those from indigenous communities. In theory, the constitutional commitment to female emancipation went well beyond demands for advances in political representation, and in 2014 these were reinforced in a 'Political Agenda from Women'. This talked of: dismantling patriarchy in cultural, symbolic, and material forms; guaranteeing a right to a life without violence; acknowledging and providing conditions in which women could exercise their sexual and reproductive rights; and enabling their economic autonomy, partly by recognizing their economic contribution and revaluating care and domestic work. Yet, in reality, Bolivia remained a deeply sexist society, with highly circumscribed abortion rights, and widespread violence against women, including in the MAS itself.

By 2014 there was also a slowdown in the economy and, partly as a result, Morales's personal popularity declined. When he sought re-election there were challenges to his right to do so, for the constitution permitted only two terms of office. The matter was referred to the Constitutional Court, now largely controlled by MAS supporters, which gave permission for the election to go ahead, securing him another presidential victory. When Morales and his supporters again sought constitutional change by allowing him to stand for a fourth term, there were still greater conflicts and 51 per cent of voters rejected the proposal in a subsequent referendum in 2016. The Constitutional Court again overturned the decision, allowing him to stand for a fourth time in October 2019.

By now ordinary citizens were voicing concerns about the state of democracy, including government control of the media and the political use of the judiciary. There were also widespread claims that the government was buying electoral support through patronage and resorting to threats and repression to divide social movements and NGOs. One of Morales's key promises in 2006 had been to crack down on corruption, but there was now discontent about its continuation at high levels. Yet there were still many sources of strength for the regime. In particular, in terms of conventional growth, the economy remained comparatively healthy and per capita income was still rising. The aftermath of the elections on 20 October 2019, which brought about the sudden end of the Morales era, was therefore wholly unexpected.

There was a febrile political atmosphere, with the election already deeply disputed and then apparent delays in counting and inconsistencies between the initial and final results. In this situation a press release on 21 October by the Organization of American States (OAS) Electoral Observation Mission was inevitably inflammatory. This expressed 'its deep concern and surprise at the drastic and hard-to-explain change in the trend of the preliminary results'. This was a catalyst for mass protests, and demonstrations and counter-demonstrations swept across the country, with increasing violence on both sides. On 10 November the head of the military asked Morales to resign and the following day he and the vice president accepted asylum in Mexico.

President Trump immediately declared that the resignation of Morales was a 'significant moment for democracy' and that 'we are now one step closer to a completely democratic, prosperous, and free Western Hemisphere'. However, many supporters of the Bolivian regime, both inside and outside the country, were adamant that this was a coup orchestrated in Washington. In time full evidence will emerge, but two points seem clear.

First, as already indicated, by 2019, there were many flaws in the system under Morales. MAS celebrated its character as an oppositional social movement without vertical systems of control and accountability, but this had facilitated the construction of a regime based on excessive personal power with inadequate judicial, legislative, and civil society accountability structures. There were also serious weaknesses in the implementation of the professed policy goals on decentralization, indigenous empowerment, equality, gender justice, and the environment. Nor did the economic model follow the 'mother earth' and *vivir bien* principles that the government proclaimed. All this meant that by the time the acute crisis erupted in October, Morales's base had fragmented. While some sectors remained as enthusiastic as ever, others had been alienated and readily accepted the claims that the leadership had been guilty of electoral manipulation.

Second, though, there were several very positive aspects in the Bolivian transformative project, which had fundamentally changed the impoverished country in less than fifteen years. In contrast, some of the forces that mobilized against Morales were both violent and racist. In particular, Luis Fernando Camacho from Santa Cruz, who emerged as a de facto leader, espoused an extreme right-wing form of Christianity and openly called for military intervention. More generally, many of those now seeking dominance sought to reverse the whole idea of a plurinational state. Any such change would undo all the progress made since 2006, and would be a further major setback for socialism in Latin America.

The balance sheet

The collapse of the Soviet bloc had ended the period in which two types of socialism had been so dominant, but this led to a situation of complexity and contradictions. On the one hand, the challenges of the New Left and later generations of protest had created a potential for new forms of socialist movement beyond the old orthodoxies. There were thus openings for innovative parties with less hierarchical and centralized organizational structures, which were open both to 'bottom-up' influences and the insights of social movements, including feminist and green thinking. On the other hand, the total dominance of the USA in the early years of this new era and its key role in promoting globalized neo-liberalism also meant that there was a narrowing of the space for alternative policies. Economic, political, and social factors would shape the ways in which each region in the world responded to these contradictory pressures.

Europe had particular difficulties in enabling socialism to realize its potential for renewal, partly because it had been the fault-line for the division between the orthodoxies of the previous era. While the enlargement of the EU certainly had some positive aspects, the rapidity of the shift in both the economic system and the geopolitics of East-Central Europe caused particular pressures. The expansion of neo-liberal policies, including by the EU itself, exacerbated the problems, particularly with the world financial crisis and the subsequent austerity measures in response to it.

However, European social democrats also tended to add to the obstacles. Perhaps because they accepted a wider liberal consensus, they generally believed that the end of the Cold War constituted a victory for human rights and democracy and that on this basis they could gradually build support for further advances. Their failure to provide robust opposition to neo-liberalism undermined their own position, making them, and European socialism in general, vulnerable to the rise of the radical right.

In the early years of the 21st century, the situation in Latin America was quite different. After years of ascendancy by right-wing regimes, and with extreme poverty and inequality in many countries, there was a very significant movement to the left in the era of the 'Pink Tide'. Benefiting from unusually favourable circumstances in the international economy, a swathe of countries took the opportunity to address some of the most extreme economic injustices. They also instituted some wider aspects of socialism initially promoted by direct action protests—particularly on gender issues.

In Venezuela, Ecuador, and Bolivia there were attempts to introduce radical forms of socialism, fusing elements of Marxism with local traditions. None of these attempts at radical transformation was wholly successful and the regime in Venezuela eventually failed catastrophically. In Bolivia, there were significant achievements as well as weaknesses, but all seemed to be brought to an abrupt end in late 2019.

In comparative terms Europe as a region, and particularly Western Europe, remained far in advance of Latin America on all the relevant measures of socioeconomic equality, democracy, and human rights. There were also very significant eruptions of protest in Europe and, as shown in the examples of Spain, Greece, and the UK, there were occasions when it seemed that there was a real potential for a regeneration of socialism. Furthermore, the setbacks in Europe are clearly less severe than those in Latin America. While the strengthening of the radical right increased inequality, and the decline in social solidarity in Europe is very serious, these changes are not comparable to the regression in Latin America as, for example, with the extremism of President Bolsonaro in Brazil.

Taken as a whole, there have been successes and failures in both regions, and their experiences provide lessons for socialism as a whole, which will be discussed in Chapter 5.

Chapter 5
Socialism today and tomorrow

This short book has provided an overview of approximately 200 years of socialism through discussion of both general trends and some case studies. It has covered many theoretical debates, some tragic episodes, and both successes and failures. This concluding chapter is divided into three sections. The first part considers the relevance of socialist ideas, the second draws out some lessons from experience, and the third looks to the future, while also arguing that we must do so by seeking to examine the past critically.

The relevance of socialist ideas

The introduction emphasized the diversity of socialism and defined it in a broad inclusive way. It suggested that socialists share a commitment to an interconnected set of values and goals. First, they are critical of the property relations of capitalism for creating societies in which life chances are distributed so unequally and they aspire to the creation of egalitarian societies. Second, they believe in the possibility of creating a different kind of society based on the values of solidarity and cooperation, for socialism is fundamentally optimistic and rejects the assumption that human beings are motivated solely by self-interest and competition. Third, they hold that conscious human agency can bring about social, political, and economic change: that human beings are subjects of history, rather than objects whose fate is entirely determined by fate, custom, or impersonal forces.

Ever since the emergence of modern socialism in the early 19th century, critics and opponents have sought to discredit these ideas. Often they have argued that the goals are 'unrealistic' because they misunderstand 'human nature' or are unworkable in practice. Considerable efforts have also been devoted to the attempt to demonstrate that socialism inevitably leads to horrific forms of tyranny. A different approach, perhaps more typical of the current era, is to suggest that socialism is simply no longer relevant. Nowadays, we are often told that new problems, such as the replacement of human beings by robots in the production process, and climate change, make socialism a doctrine of the past. What kind of response can be made to such criticisms?

In my view, it is dishonest and counterproductive for socialists to avoid or minimize the negative features in the record or to assume that the doctrine has all the answers, and these points will be further elaborated later in this chapter. However, there is also much reason for confidence about the continuing relevance of socialism in the current era.

Since the critique of capitalist inequality has been so central in socialism, this is the starting point for any discussion of its relevance today. Inequality is inherent in capitalism, and, as discussed in Chapter 1, in this respect Marx made an indispensable contribution with his explanations of the reasons for class inequality and conflict, and also of the inherent tendency of capitalism to involve periods of crisis. Thomas Piketty recently complemented this in *Capital in the Twenty-First Century*, which included an immense amount of statistical evidence on the trajectory of capitalist economies over time, and also contained a compelling central argument. For he argued that the return on capital was always greater than the rate of growth. This meant that inherited wealth and returns on assets would always increase faster than income earned through wages. Moreover, without government intervention, the gap was bound to grow.

This insight, and the evidence of trends, demonstrates the continuing relevance of socialism. As the *World Inequality Report 2018* shows, during the neoliberal era since the 1970s, a long-term historical decline in inequality in most parts of the world over the previous half-century has been reversed, with an increase in income inequality almost everywhere.

This has been particularly striking in the USA, the leader in global liberalization, where the share of income going to the bottom 50 per cent of the population collapsed while those at the top experienced a boom. By 2014 the share of national income going to the top 1 per cent of adults (20.2 per cent) was thus much larger than that earned by the bottom 50 per cent (12.5 per cent). In the UK, which adopted a more radical form of market-driven capitalism than most other West European states, the regression in terms of inequality has also been very marked.

There have also been dramatic increases in inequality since formerly communist systems adopted forms of capitalism. Whereas the top 10 per cent and bottom 50 per cent both had 27 per cent of national income in China in 1978, by 2015 the share of the former had increased to 42 per cent while the latter decreased to 15 per cent. In Russia, the change was still more rapid and extreme. In 1989, the share of national income going to the bottom 50 per cent was 30 per cent, but in the second decade of the 21st century it was only 20 per cent, while in the same period the share of the top 1 per cent rose from around 25 per cent to over 45 per cent. This meant that inequality levels became somewhat higher than they were before the Russian revolution in 1917.

Finally, there is immense global inequality. Certainly, some of the most extreme inequality is within particular parts of the Global South, particularly in Brazil, the Middle East, and South Africa.

But the most extreme poverty is still in the developing countries, above all in Sub-Saharan Africa, which remain locked into a subordinate position in the international economy. Here the poverty is that of absolute destitution—the lack of food, drinking water, basic sanitation, healthcare, and education. Meanwhile, during 2018 billionaire fortunes increased daily by 12 per cent a day, while the wealth of the 3.8 billion poorest people declined by 11 per cent. The wealth of the twenty-six richest billionaires equalled that of the poorest half of the world population.

Global inequality may appear more urgent than the gap between the wealthy and the poor in the rich countries, but it is misleading to set one kind of inequality against another. In their highly influential book, *The Spirit Level*, Kate Pickett and Richard Wilkinson argued that all income groups flourish to a greater extent in more equal societies in terms of life expectation, health, and general well-being.

Statistical data provide concrete evidence on measurable indicators of social and economic inequalities and these are closely related to other crucial forms of inequality, including those in gender and ethnicity. However, socialists have never confined their case to these dimensions alone, but have also condemned inequality because it allocates the possibilities of human development so unevenly and arbitrarily. Behind the statistics are also the injustice of unequal power and unequal possibilities for intellectual and artistic creativity and personal fulfilment. There are also other highly significant aspects in terms of the *political* consequences of sharp changes in socioeconomic distribution. While it would be oversimplified to attribute the growth of right-wing nationalism and extremism in Russia, the USA, or the UK entirely to these factors, they are certainly important aspects of the explanation.

As already noted, it is sometimes suggested that socialism is outdated in relation to the other most pressing problems of our era. As shown in Chapter 3, socialists are still at a relatively early stage in addressing the multiple dimensions of climate change and cannot be satisfied by their progress, but at least they have recognized the crucial importance of making a transition to a sustainable economy. Furthermore, the socialist emphasis on cooperation and solidarity, both within and between societies and states, will be essential in the crucial task of bringing about global solutions. In contrast, capitalism has generally remained wedded to a traditional growth model within competing states, often fostering and expanding the fossil fuel industries. In many cases, both the most damaging industries, with particular responsibility for global warming, and the leaders of some major states continue to deny, against the overwhelming weight of evidence, that humanity is largely responsible for climate change.

The argument that technological progress, rather than capitalism, is now the threat to the future of employment is equally fallacious. In this view, the advances in information technology and robotics have already made numerous workers redundant and in future will transform the world of work so fundamentally that much human labour will be deskilled or unnecessary. There is no doubt that we are in a new era of rapid technological transformation, but socialists deny that there is anything inevitable about the way in which it is used and its impact upon the lives of working people. Under capitalism, calculations of profitably will be the major factor in decisions about utilization. However, the advances could have positive, rather than negative effects, if used to expand freedom and human agency.

Yet however relevant socialism may be *in theory*, it faces problems unless sufficient people *perceive* it in this way. It is therefore constantly necessary to make the socialist case in the attempt to win support. Thus, to return to the fundamental issue of inequality, recognition of the basic facts and trends is clearly insufficient. In general, people know that poverty and inequality exist on a massive scale, but this does not make them socialists.

In general, it is far easier to make the case against poverty than against inequality. Even the richest and most powerful corporate directors no doubt feel deeply uncomfortable when confronted with pictures of starving people and accept that this kind of poverty should not be allowed. However, they are much less likely to accept equality as a value or to agree that inequality is embedded in the nature and dynamics of capitalism. They are often more inclined to share some of the general assumptions used to discredit socialism—for example that inequality is an inevitable part of the human condition. From the 1970s onwards, such beliefs were reinforced through the role of neo-liberal ideology in cultivating individualist notions and aspirations, and in promoting the idea that progress depends upon rewarding those with extra talent, energy, and ambition.

Socialists would expect the very wealthy and powerful to promote such ideas, but might hope that the majority of the population would favour equality or at least gradual progress towards greater egalitarianism. However, this is not necessarily so, partly because political and social institutions and the media are generally favourable to capitalist society and play a key role in influencing opinion. This is one aspect of the more general arguments discussed in Chapter 3 about the moulding of consciousness so as to stifle dissent. Thus, in a somewhat extreme form, Marcuse argued that all the influences of modern industrial capitalism combine to create a single outlook in which the overwhelming majority can no longer even see the possibility of alternatives. More persuasively, Gramsci argued that the combination of coercion and social and cultural influences produced a capitalist hegemony.

Yet it is also important not to exaggerate the impact of all the pressures towards individualism, even when governments and economic elites propagate the idea that unregulated capitalism promotes freedom for all. Thus between 1990 and 2008 opinion across the EU as a whole, and particularly amongst the most vulnerable groups, increasingly inclined towards greater support for some forms of egalitarianism and social protection. However, even though most people may resist the most extreme ideas of competitive individualism, this does not mean that they embrace a socialist notion of equality.

Many liberals and social democrats have endorsed the much weaker notion of 'equality of opportunity'. This holds that there is no need for equality as a goal as long as those from poorer backgrounds have a real chance to rise in society. The assumption is that enhancing the openings for upward social mobility for those with particular merit is sufficient. Most socialists would agree that, if this were possible, it would be preferable to a society in which class, caste, or wealth wholly determined life chances. But the sociologist Zygmunt Bauman (1925–2017) provided a succinct refutation of the claims for 'equality of opportunity':

> 'Equality of opportunity' means, in fact, equal chances to make the best of inequality; indeed, equality of opportunity is an empty notion unless the social setting to which it refers is structured on a basis of inequality. Thus the very use of the term, in a sense, sanctifies and accepts as a constant predicament what socialism is bent on annihilating.

Nevertheless, there are conceptual difficulties in the idea of equality and opponents of socialism often exaggerate its implications in order to discredit it.

Absolute equality between human beings will, of course, never be achieved. People are different in their talents, energies, interests, strength, and so on. In his *Critique of the Gotha Programme* (1875), even Marx accepted that individuals were unequal, for 'they would not be different individuals if they were not unequal'. However, equality as a core value in socialism does not imply an unrealizable goal. Rather, it suggests the aspiration to create a society in which all have the possibility of fulfilment and in which life chances are not allocated by structural inequalities in social, economic, and political power. Of course, even this is a highly ambitious goal, but it can be used to evaluate and criticize societies and to push and prod them to become more equal. In relation to capitalism, this involves calling for constant inroads into the privileges of ownership rather than limited reforms and palliatives. Similarly, on a world scale, socialists must continue to press for trade and development policies that provide constant increases in the demonstrable benefits for poorer countries and groups.

The other core values of cooperation and social solidarity are closely connected to that of equality and, once again, socialists need to demonstrate their continued relevance. It is not difficult to counter an emphasis on individual self-interest as an adequate explanation of behaviour. As much recent research has demonstrated, cooperation has been an essential aspect of human survival and achievement throughout history, and is evident in all spheres of activity. However, the idea of social solidarity is different.

While cooperation normally involves common action within a group, social solidarity involves a sense of commitment to a much larger population of unknown people. Historically, socialist and labour solidarity have been powerful ideas. These involve active support for others in their fights against aspects of capitalism even when one's own direct interests are not affected. Social solidarity holds that people have a connection with wider society and that the public good transcends the claims of individual self-interest when there is a conflict between the two.

As shown in Chapter 4, the rise of neo-liberalism undermined the ideologies, institutions, and communities that sustained both socialist and social solidarity, making the task of persuasion more difficult. Yet socialists may also point to negative features of contemporary society in order to reinforce their arguments. Many people regret the absence of social solidarity or community, believing that there was once a greater sense of shared values and that crime, drugs, violence, and the constant breakdown of relationships have something to do with the excessive individualism of contemporary life. This is also the case with the increasing problem of loneliness, particularly among the growing ageing populations. In these and many other areas there is widespread recognition of the need for adequate social provision.

Socialists can also insist that the alleged antithesis between the individual and the community is false and that cooperation and solidarity are also means to individual self-realization. Yet they need to demonstrate that redistribution and regulation are crucial for social solidarity. For this assumes that part of the total wealth created by any society must be devoted to collective provision in such spheres as health, housing, and education. Those who favour capitalism may contest this, for example, by arguing that the most productive should keep the wealth because they have earned it, or that social redistribution undermines incentives to enterprise and rewards the idle. Social solidarity also runs counter to the appeal to individual self-interest that has been cultivated, for this promotes the view that only direct beneficiaries need to pay for such services.

Stressing the crucial importance of the benefits of solidarity for society as a whole and, more generally, reaffirming the other core values of the doctrine, are essential elements in refuting the gloomy verdict of Ralf Dahrendorf in 1990, quoted in Chapter 4, that 'socialism is dead'.

Lessons

It is equally necessary to look self-critically at the record of socialism. What lessons should have been learned?

First, socialism of the future must grapple with complex issues about power and democracy within both its own organizations and the wider institutions in which it operates. The notion of equality in socialist thought has never solely concerned material resources, but has also referred to power relations. It should now be clear to all that communist dictatorships, whether in the past or present, wholly contradict political equality and can never provide adequate forms of cooperation and solidarity. Dictatorship must be rejected, with democracy viewed as a central element of socialism. Yet Chapter 4 suggested only limited progress in this respect.

It is, of course, much easier to stress the importance of socialist democracy than to conceptualize it, let alone apply it in practice. In general, social democratic parties and trade unions have been hierarchical and bureaucratic and, although Sweden had achievements in many areas, it did not fully overcome such problems. Similarly, while Cuba clearly had many successes, it was never genuinely democratic either within the party or in the relationships between society and the state.

Nor have attempts to move away from the previously dominant forms of socialism resolved the problems of effecting a democratic socialist transformation. In Latin America there has been a strong tradition of social movements, but their democratic interconnections with parties, wider society, and the state have not been adequately demonstrated. The Chávez regime in Venezuela degenerated into a system of charismatic leadership and popular mobilization without any effective forms of democratic control. The Bolivian regime was also flawed as a new model for socialism. In theory the MAS was a social movement rather than a conventional party, but it lacked robust forms of internal control and accountability or even channels for genuinely independent participation. Leadership domination was therefore also a feature of Bolivia under Morales.

In Europe since the late 19th century there has been a strong emphasis on socialist parties as the main agency of change. In general, social democracy and other parties of the left now believe in democracy and human rights and, in principle, accept the need for participation by civil society movements and rank-and-file members. However, this does not mean that there has been significant progress in achieving a satisfactory relationship between social movement activism and political parties.

Attempts to build viable long-term organizations from direct action protests have been problematic. Non-hierarchical movements, for example in climate change campaigns, have sometimes had a major impact in the short term. The action by Extinction Rebellion in London during Easter 2019 certainly raised awareness of the issues and the worldwide international school strike movement for climate justice in September made it difficult for politicians to ignore the problems. However, making such movements effective agencies of change in the long term is a far more difficult task. The trajectory of Podemos in Spain demonstrates the problems in trying to combine a bottom-up locally based direct action movement with a party based on electoral and governmental ambitions.

At the same time socialists will always insist that democracy, as understood and practised within the liberal and capitalist framework, is insufficient. Even successful election to office leaves many of the most powerful economic, political, and social institutions beyond control, and, as demonstrated by the Trump era in the USA, constitutional safeguards against the abuse of power may be far less robust than generally assumed.

In my view, socialism requires an institutional system with a dispersal of power at all levels, in a multi-party system. However, this does not mean confining political activity to parties or established institutional channels. Social movements have demonstrated the effectiveness of single-issue campaigns and, through forms of intersectionalism, often construct valuable alliances. Similarly, trade unions remain crucial to defend and promote the interests of the working classes. All this suggests that a 21st-century socialist concept of democracy should seek to incorporate aspects of both the representative and participatory traditions.

Yet the democratic commitment can seem a little bland when right-wing forces are often so hypocritical—simultaneously extolling the virtues of democracy while using all forms of repression to defeat the left. This does not justify any weakening in the commitment to democracy as an integral part of socialism, but it necessitates constant vigilance, exposure, and opposition to the double standards in the practices of capitalist democracies.

A second lesson from past experience is that socialists still need to develop viable economic strategies. In both Cuba and Sweden economic success underpinned the social advances, but these were threatened when the economy faltered. This was demonstrated once again by the experience of the 'Pink Tide' in Latin America, when the downturn of the economy by 2015 quickly led to a return to the right in several countries. In particular, the radical programme in Venezuela collapsed in chaos largely as a result of economic mismanagement. In Europe too, weaknesses in economic policy had highly negative effects. In this respect the failure of social democracy was crucial in undermining its own potential and opening up new opportunities for the rise of the radical right. Such evidence reinforces the argument that socialists need to devote considerable efforts to develop practical approaches for an alternative form of economy.

Towards the end of the Cold War, when the inefficiencies of Soviet central planning were starkly evident, many socialists began to consider alternative ways of combining plans and markets. The debate was initiated by Alec Nove in *The Economics of Feasible Socialism* in 1983 and attracted a great deal of interest, with many different versions advocated—some of which veered more towards the plan and some more towards the market. There has also been interest in a variety of different forms of ownership, including cooperatives, decentralized public ownership, and mixed companies of both private and public capital. A further variation has been in schemes to use the state's purchasing power to provide support for ventures with growth and innovation potential.

However, such ideas do not always question the fundamental assumption in capitalist economic theory: that the primary criterion for evaluating success is the rate of growth in output. Yet a key aspect of the green challenge to socialism has been to incorporate the idea of sustainability into economic thought and, with the overwhelming threat of climate change, this is now the imperative need of the era. It is therefore no longer sufficient simply to observe that attempts to institute forms of socialism have been dependent upon maintaining conventionally successful economies, for these have also wasted resources, causing irreversible ecological and planetary damage, and have been unsustainable.

It is now urgent to devise practical ways of combining long-term socialist priorities with sustainability. Considerable thought is now being devoted to such ideas, as, for example, in the Green New Deal proposals and many local level experiments, but these are still at a comparatively early stage. Furthermore, there are vast theoretical and practical difficulties in securing the necessary progress on a global level when the key decisions remain national.

This leads to a third lesson: further thought needs to be devoted to the question of the *level* at which socialism is envisaged, for this is now more complex than ever. In general, the early socialists, anarchists, and, more recently, green thinkers have sought to introduce their projects through decentralized communities, while communists and social democrats tended towards centralization at the level of the state. The problems in both approaches have been constant. Decentralization implies the possibilities of greater control, accountability, and sensitivity to local needs, but fails to explain how to secure any kind of equalization between areas with widely different existing resource levels, or how to handle highly conservative or reactionary local power systems. Centralization suggests a way of tackling the latter problems, but at the expense of local democracy.

The increasing internationalization of the economy has exacerbated these problems. If states (or, at least, most states) no longer wield sufficient power to bring about radical change, the traditional terms of the debate about level are anachronistic, and need to be recast in relation to the transnational, national, regional, and local. Nor is it even clear that this territorial approach is adequate, for power operates in different ways in different spheres, suggesting that functional divisions also need to be considered.

Such debates have been particularly important within Europe and, during the 1980s and 1990s, many socialists believed that the EU might provide a framework in which a resolution of the problems would be possible. For example, there was support for the idea of decentralization in a federal or semi-federal system with the aim of ensuring that each decision was taken at the most appropriate level. However, any movement in a federal direction is constrained by the contemporary impasse in the EU, fuelled by the impact of neo-liberalism and austerity, the backlash against migration, the Brexit crisis, and the rise of right-wing extremism. Furthermore, many socialists are now opposed to further European integration, arguing that it is simply a vehicle for capitalism. Others are equally adamant in insisting that it remains a necessary framework for progress. In my own view, the EU, though with greater democratization and decentralization, is essential for enhancing socialist values of peace and cooperation, and could be a potential model for regional integration in other parts of the world, including Latin America. Such debates about level also raise the more general questions of nationalism and internationalism.

As noted in Chapter 1, socialists have not always been internationalist in outlook. Some have regarded their own state so positively that they have effectively embraced nationalism, while others have concentrated on the domestic construction of socialism without taking much interest in international developments. In many respects, the collapse of the Second International in 1914 was not simply a historical episode, but reflects a continuing phenomenon. For elements of nationalism are so deeply embedded in social consciousness that, when faced with an existential crisis, many socialists will rally to their own state.

Against this, I would argue that there are overwhelming reasons, both theoretical and practical, for maintaining that 21st-century socialism must be internationalist. Yet contemporary developments also demonstrate the dangers of socialists assuming that there would be a progressive weakening of national, religious, cultural, and ethnic identities. Following a combination of Enlightenment and Marxist traditions, there has been a tendency to regard these as pre-modern forms of consciousness that will be replaced by secularism, and, eventually, socialism. However, 21st-century socialists will need to accept that particular and multiple identities have enduring importance for people. It is necessary to ensure that socialist doctrine is both compatible with this fact and perceived as being compatible.

Putting internationalism into practice is still more difficult. Opposition to imperialism in the shape of formal empires appears straightforward, but socialists have not always succeeded in converting an abstract internationalism into concrete policies. The global dimension may be supremely important for socialist progress, but it is also the most complex, and there are no simple solutions. The goal must be to advance towards equality between countries and peoples and to attempt to construct forms of transnational solidarity and cooperation. Progress in these spheres would be difficult in any circumstances, but the problems are vastly increased by the distribution of global power and the

12. Anti-capitalist protesters outside the Bank of England in London, 2009.

current opposition of the leaders in the USA, Russia, China, and India to any international regimes that might limit their autonomy. Global social movements share the insistence of socialists that 'another world is possible', but advancing towards its realization may be slow and painful (see Figure 12). Many urgent problems, above all that of climate change, require global solutions, but the conversion of theory into practice will be immensely difficult, particularly given the power of the interests that seek to prevent the necessary transformations.

This leads to a more general final issue: the need for honest recognition of the fact that the current situation is difficult and that formidable problems lie ahead. How should socialists face the future?

Facing the future

In recognition of the current problems, there is a tendency among some socialists to become pessimistic. This is perhaps hardly surprising. In many countries where forms of socialism were previously relatively strong, it seems to have crumbled, and the rulers of the strongest states in the world have turned to aggressive nationalism and hostility to both liberal and socialist ideas. Furthermore, there are new dangers, with right-wing leaders in the USA and Russia using social media and the internet to plant 'fake news' with simplistic messages, again undermining progressive ideas and institutions.

Yet pessimism can never be an effective response to difficulties and, if socialists adopt this outlook, they disarm themselves in the battle to persuade others of the continuing relevance of the doctrine. It is, however, equally misguided and counter-productive to pretend that all is well and that the apparent problems are illusory.

Perhaps paradoxically, I hold that the starting point for facing the future is to look back to the past with a rigorous and honest historical perspective. This tells us that there has never been any linear progression towards socialism, for advances have always been uneven. On the eve of the First World War, the parties of the Second International were confident that capitalism would end in the near future. In fact, there was the appalling slaughter of millions of people, above all of the working classes. After 1917, the Bolshevik Revolution inspired communists throughout the world to believe that the transformation in Russia constituted the birth of a new world, while social democrats asserted that socialism could be constructed peacefully and constitutionally. Instead, there was fascism, Stalinism, another devastating war, and Nazi genocide. Most socialists may have hoped and believed that there would be a constant march onward and upward towards their goals, but the reality has always been more complex.

History should also provide safeguards against any tendency to believe in the myth of a 'golden age'. Certainly there are currently major challenges for socialism, but looking at previous eras through rose tinted spectacles can be dangerous as well as inaccurate. To suggest that things were previously better from a socialist perspective generally implies that socialism itself was better. It is only a short step from any such claim to the conclusion that fundamental and crippling injustices in the past were simply blemishes. At its most extreme, this could imply that Stalin's death camps and arbitrary executions were simply regrettable excesses rather than monstrous crimes. Similar problems arise in relation to less obviously objectionable assertions. For example, social democracy during the 1950s and 1960s was clearly generally more effective than in the inter-war period because it maintained full employment and effective social security systems. But simply to extol it as a 'success' is to disregard the generally sexist, racist, and Eurocentric aspects of its assumptions and practices. Socialism has advanced in these latter respects, and it is more helpful to consider it holistically, by recognizing progress as well as problems.

A different but equally wrong-headed stance lies in a simplistic attitude to doctrine. Instead of accepting a diversity of approaches and theories and thinking about these in a self-critical way, there is sometimes a tendency to treat ideas as dogma. This can lead to a vehement affirmation that one approach can overcome all impediments to progress. Many sectarian Marxists have advanced arguments of this kind, implying that all attempts to institute socialism have been 'betrayals' and that the future would be bright if the 'correct' line were implemented. Claims of this kind have been made ever since the Bolshevik Revolution, but often alienate more potential socialists than they attract. Others have implied that other variants of socialism, whether old or new, contain 'the solution'. I agree that many strands of socialist doctrine, including Marxism, may now contribute to the future successes of socialism, but doubt whether any of them individually holds the key. Socialism is not self-contained and it cannot explain everything, but it comprises interconnected values, theories, and practices that define both an outlook on the world and a commitment to change it.

Interpretations of the contemporary situation are inevitably subjective and gazing into a crystal ball is of limited value, but there are surely positive as well as negative tendencies and trends. While social media and the internet provide additional means of control for the rich and powerful, they have also brought about international awareness of social, economic, and political oppression and injustice for oppositional movements. These are able to mobilize extremely quickly and effectively, both nationally and internationally. Furthermore, while there may be an apparent decline of socialism in some countries, there are often contradictory trends—sometimes in surprising places.

In this respect, the situation in the United States has been remarkable, for in 2016 Bernie Sanders came very close to securing the Democratic Party nomination as presidential candidate although he openly described himself as a socialist. Not only have the Democratic Socialists of America recently undergone a revival, particularly with the prominence of Alexandria Ocasio-Cortez, but in 2018 one survey showed that, amongst young people, there was greater support for socialism—now widely understood in a rather loose, open sense, with equality as the key value—than for capitalism. This had been almost inconceivable in the USA for seventy years, for socialism had long been equated with the Soviet Union. Under President Donald Trump, US policy certainly turned sharply to the right, but it also became far more polarized.

Such shifts demonstrated that change is often rapid and unpredictable. This is related to the issue of political volatility, which is a feature of the current era, leading to uncertainties and often a sense of insecurity. This partly explains the tendency for people to rally to strong leadership and right-wing movements, but the constant mutations in the current era also offer a basis for hope about the future.

Ever since the birth of the New Left in the mid-1950s, socialism has been enriched and decentred and this process has gathered pace more recently. There are always fears that new challenges will simply cause fragmentation and disintegration. For the dominant orthodoxies in the second half of the last century, both feminist and green ideas and movements thus appeared threatening. But this sense of danger was never necessary and both the 'feminization' of work, organizations, power, and personal relationships, and green approaches, are now widely accepted as integral parts of socialism. The challenges to established ideas about power and organization might appear still more unsettling.

In recent times, there has been constant disruption of long held assumptions about institutions, structures, and organizations. In particular, it has been customary to think about power as structured in some way in institutions, but it will become increasingly necessary to accept that it inheres in fluid local, regional, national, and transnational interactions. The challenge will be to find ways of taking effective action in a constantly mutating complexity.

This will no doubt need to recognize both the importance of defining appropriate levels for different types of policy decision (as in the earlier discussion of the EU), while accepting that these will not be static. For example, urban centres in many parts of the world have experienced similar negative effects of austerity, and have drawn on local sources of power and initiative to counter them. This so-called 'New Muncipalism' has led to a transnational sharing of lessons learned. At the same time, however, it will also need to be recognized that many meaningful forms of socialist activity have little direct relationship with traditional notions of power and control. No one would suggest that a city or local community can transform international policies, but they may be the key locations for cultural activity, and the development of socialist consciousness. The overall impact of all this may be highly significant, particularly when experiences are shared transnationally.

Closely related to this is the fact that socialists can no longer assume continuity in their own organizations. Throughout much of the 20th century, they devoted much effort to creating parties of a particular kind, normally associated with trade unions, and these also developed specific traditions of bureaucracy and procedure. Yet the world has clearly changed. Strong allegiance to parties is generally in decline, as is identification with a traditionally defined socialist programme, and the patterns of work that originally dominated the ethos of trade unions now exist only for a minority of working-class people.

At the same time, some of the most salient issues, which generate mass protests and forms of direct action, tend to develop outside, and sometimes against, any form of party. Of course, this does not mean socialists no longer need parties and trade unions, but there is a need for constant adaptation and change, not by jettisoning key principles, but by constant renewal and engagement with wider social movements. This climate of fluidity may be unsettling, but it also offers opportunities.

What, then, is the basis for optimism about the future of socialism? In an earlier era of pessimism, many endorsed a claim by the Italian Marxist theorist Antonio Gramsci that the appropriate outlook was 'pessimism of the intelligence, optimism of the will'. However, a later socialist thinker, Ralph Miliband (1924–94), regarded this as an 'exceedingly bad slogan'. It simultaneously suggested that reason dictated the conviction that nothing was likely to work out as it should, that defeat was more likely than success, but that socialists must 'nevertheless strive towards it . . . in a mood of resolute despair'. But this was implausible, for there was not likely to be much striving if intelligence suggested the enterprise was 'vain, hopeless, doomed'.

However, he equally adamantly rejected the idea at the other extreme—of 'an historical escalator' inevitably carrying those on the left 'to the promised land of an easy-to-realize socialism'. This is surely an appropriate balance.

There is one final point. This book has argued that socialism is not a single doctrine and I believe that all its traditions have a place, even at the risk of eclecticism. For example, Marxists have often tended to put forward a framework purporting to provide both an overall theoretical explanation for the social sciences and a guide to action. However, there are strong arguments for disaggregating Marxist theory and combining elements of it with other traditions.

As a critique of capitalism, which explains its structures, dynamics, and propensity to crisis, Marx's work remains unsurpassed, and it also provides compelling insights into a whole range of social, political, and philosophical debates. Yet there are areas in which his contribution seems minimal or unhelpful, for example, in relation to the nature of socialism within democracy or as an ethical guide. Yet if Marx should not be treated with reverence as a prophet, it is equally inappropriate to ignore his work or to dismiss it. Only purist Marxists and anti-Marxists will refuse to accept that the strongest elements of the theory can be combined with ethical and democratic ideas derived from other traditions.

Much of the contribution of these traditions has been implicit in the discussion above—for example, in the differing ideas of centralist and decentralist views about the level at which socialism should be constructed, and in debates about the relative merits of parties or direct action in transforming society. A synthesis between these different traditions may not be possible, and tensions will continue to exist within the socialist project. For example, the anarchist distrust of states, parties, and leaders is surely valuable. As Proudhon put it, both eloquently and provocatively:

To be governed is to be watched over, inspected, spied on, directed, legislated at, regulated, docketed, indoctrinated, preached at, controlled, assessed, weighed, censored, ordered about, by men who have neither the right nor the knowledge nor the virtue . . . That's government, that's its justice, that's its morality!

However, change will also depend upon the use of public power and upon practical thinkers who concentrate on finding solutions to problems. This approach formed an important part of Swedish social democracy at its peak. This is the mentality of incrementalists, who keep their feet planted firmly on the ground and are sceptical about grand projects of transformation.

Nevertheless in a world beset by so many fundamental problems, including inequality and poverty, visions of the future are also vital and it is important to remember that many gains that are now taken for granted were once seen as utopian. As Oscar Wilde wrote:

A map of the world that does not include Utopia is not worth even glancing at, for it leaves out the one country at which Humanity is always landing. And when Humanity lands there, it looks out, and, seeing a better country, sets sail. Progress is the realisation of Utopias.

References

Chapter 1: Socialist traditions

The definition of socialism in the London Co-operative magazine is quoted in G. Lichtheim, *A Short History of Socialism* (London: Fontana, 1975), p. 45.

Owen's description of the people when he arrived in New Lanark is from *A New View of Society*, Second Essay (1816), reproduced on Marxists Internet Archive <https://www.marxists.org/reference/subject/economics/owen/ch02.htm>

Owen's generalization about training in his Fourth Essay in *A New View of Society* is from <https://www.marxists.org/reference/subject/economics/owen/ch04.htm>

The quotation from Proudhon's *What is Property?* is in J. Joll, *The Anarchists* (London: Eyre and Spottiswoode, 1964), p. 71.

The quotation from Bakunin on the workers in Italy is from his *Œuvres*, vol. V, quoted in Joll 1964, p. 92.

Bakunin's condemnation of communism was in 1868 at a meeting of the League of Peace and Freedom, quoted in Joll 1964, p. 107.

The statement by the anarchists in Switzerland was in 1871, quoted in Joll 1964, p. 105.

Preface of *A Contribution to the Critique of Political Economy* in David McLellan, *Karl Marx: Selected Writings* (Oxford: Oxford University Press, 1977), pp. 388–91.

The Communist Manifesto, McLellan, *Karl Marx* 1977, pp. 222–47.

Donald Sassoon, *One Hundred Years of Socialism* (London: Taurus, 1996).

Lenin, *What is to Be Done? Burning Questions of our Movement* (1902),

Marxists Internet Archive <https://www.marxists.org/archive/lenin/works/1901/witbd/index.htm>

Lenin, *The State and Revolution* (1917), <https://www.marxists.org/archive/lenin/works/1917/staterev/>.

Rosa Luxemburg, 'Organizational Questions of the Russian Social Democracy' (1904), <https://www.marxists.org/archive/luxemburg/1904/questions-rsd/ch01.htm>.

Leon Trotsky, *Our Political Tasks* (1904), <https://www.marxists.org/archive/trotsky/1904/tasks/>.

Chapter 2: Cuban communism and Swedish social democracy

Per Albin Hansson on the 'people's home' is quoted in Tim Tilton, *The Political Theory of Swedish Social Democracy: Through Welfare State to Socialism* (Oxford: Clarendon Press, 1991), p. 259.

The statistics for female participation rates are in Jacob Mincer, 'Intercountry Comparisons of Labour Force Trends and of Related Developments: An Overview', *Journal of Labor Economics*, 1985, 3 (1), p. 52.

The five central themes characterizing Swedish Social Democracy are in Tilton, pp. 257–69.

The statistics on Swedish social expenditure are from Francis Castles, 'The Growth of the Post-war Public Expenditure State: Long-Term Trajectories and Recent Trends', TranState working papers, No. 35 Univ., *Sonderforschungsbereich* 597. 2006, pp. 15–19.

For Swedish taxation rates, see Mikael Stenkula, 'Swedish Taxation in a 150 Year Perspective', *Nordic Tax Journal*, 2014.

Henry Milner, *Sweden: Social Democracy in Practice* (Oxford: Oxford University Press, 1990), pp. 54–84.

The statistics on the decline in blue-collar jobs and SAP dominance are from Monika Arvidsson, 'Changes to the "Swedish Model": Trade Unions under Pressure', *Friedrich Ebert Stiftung*, August 2014; and Göran Therborn, 'Twilight of Swedish Social Democracy', *New Left Review*, 111, 2018.

For the rise on educational inequality, see Kajsa Yang Hansen and Jan-Eric Gustafsson, 'Identifying the Key Source of Deteriorating Educational Equity in Sweden between 1998 and 2014', *International Journal of Educational Research*, 93, 2019.

'Gender Equality Index 2017', 'Measuring Gender Equality in the European Union 2005–2015', European Institute for Gender Equality, 2017.

Unless otherwise stated, the statistics on Cuba from the late 1950s until 1993 are from Susan Eckstein, *Back from the Future: Cuba under Castro* (Princeton: Princeton University Press, 1994).

For statistics and analysis of the impact of the economic crisis, see Jorge Pérez-López, 'The Cuban Economic Crisis of the 1990s and the External Sector', *Association for the Study of the Cuban Economy*, 30 November 1998. <https://www.ascecuba.org/asce_proceedings/the-cuban-economic-crisis-of-the-1990s-and-the-external-sector/>.

For analysis of Raúl Castro's economic reforms, see Ricardo Torres Pérez, 'Updating the Cuban Economy: The First 10 Years', *Social Research*, 84 (2) Summer 2017.

For acknowledgement by officials of the low rate of growth in 2018, see Richard Feinberg, 'Cuba's Economy after Raúl Castro: A Tale of Three Worlds', *Foreign Policy at Brookings*, February 2018 <https://www.brookings.edu/research/cubas-economy-after-raul-castro-a-tale-of-three-worlds/>.

The figure on startling differentials between the beneficiaries of tourism and those on state salaries is from Katrin Hansing, 'Race and Inequality in the New Cuba', *Social Research*, 84 (2) Summer 2017, p. 335.

The statistics on the decline in Communist Party membership are in William M. LeoGrande, 'Updating Cuban Socialism', *Social Research*, 84 (2) Summer 2017, p. 374.

ECLAC (Economic Commission for Latin America and the Caribbean), Social Panorama of Latin America, 2016, <https://www.cepal.org/en/pressreleases/eclac-high-levels-inequality-latin-america-constitute-obstacle-sustainable-development>.

This analysis of the consultation on the referendum is in Jon Lee Anderson, 'Cuba's Next Transformation', *New York Times*, 9 January 2019. <https://www.nytimes.com/2019/01/05/opinion/sunday/cubas-next-transformation.html>.

Chapter 3: New Lefts—enrichment and fragmentation

The number of Occupy protests in 2011 was compiled from verified news reports in *The Guardian*, 14 November 2011, <https://www.

theguardian.com/news/datablog/2011/oct/17/occupy-protests-world-list-map.>.

The critique of Marx's theory of the sources of women's oppression is based on Sheila Rowbotham, 'Dear Mr Marx: A Letter from a Socialist Feminist', in Leo Panitch and Colin Leys (eds), *Socialist Register 1998* (London: Merlin Press, 1998).

For Lenin's remarks on communist women discussing sexual matters, see Clara Zetkin, 'Lenin on the *Women's Question*', Marxists Internet Archive, <https://www.marxists.org/archive/zetkin/1925/lenin/zetkin2.htm>.

The statistics about children in crèches and kindergartens in East Germany and the party statement about women are in Geoff Eley, *Forging Democracy: The History of the Left in Europe, 1850–2000* (Oxford: Oxford University Press, 2002), p. 324.

On the role of women in 1968, see Eley, *Forging Democracy*, p. 366.

Chandra Talpade Mohanty, 'Under Western Eyes: Feminist Scholarship and Colonial Discourses', *Boundary* 2 12 (3) 1984.

Kimberle Crenshaw, 'Demarginalizing the Intersection of Race and Sex: A Black Feminist Critique of Antidiscrimination Doctrine, Feminist Theory and Antiracist Politics', *The University of Chicago Legal Forum* 1989, 1.

The estimates of the numbers on the Women's March are from Kaveh Waddell, 'The Exhausting Work of Tallying America's Largest Protest', *The Atlantic*, 23 January 2017, <https://www.theatlantic.com/technology/archive/2017/01/womens-march-protest-count/514166/>.

Cinzia Arruzza, Tithi Bhattacharya, and Nancy Fraser, *Feminism for the 99%: A Manifesto* (London and New York: Verso, 2019).

The IPCC special report of 2018 is *Global Warming of 1.5 °C* <https://www.ipcc.ch/sr15/>.

Michael Jacobs, *Green Social Democracy*, Fabian Society, 21 January 2013, <https://fabians.org.uk/green-social-democracy/> and 'Green Social Democracy can Rescue Capitalism from Itself', *New Statesman*, 19 January 2013, <https://www.newstatesman.com/politics/2013/01/green-social-democracy-can-rescue-capitalism-itself>.

Party of European Socialists, 'Fair Free Sustainable: The Progressive Europe We Want', 7–8 December 2018, <https://www.pes.eu/export/sites/default/.galleries/Documents-gallery/Resolution_Enviroment_MR_NoCrops.pdf_2063069294.pdf>.

A Green New Deal, Joined-Up Policies to Solve the Triple Crunch of the Credit Crisis, Climate Change and High Oil Prices, New Economics Foundation, 2008, <https://neweconomics.org/2008/07/green-new-deal>.

Ann Pettifor, *The Case for the Green New Deal* (London and New York: Verso 2019).

H.Res.109—Recognizing the Duty of the Federal Government to Create a Green New Deal, 116th Congress (2019–2020) Introduced by Alexandria Ocasio-Cortez, 7 February 2019, <https://www.congress.gov/bill/116th-congress/house-resolution/109/text>.

Rudolf Bahro, *Socialism and Survival* (London: Heretic Books, 1982).

David Sandalow, *Guide to Chinese Climate Policy 2018*, Columbia/SIPA, Center on Global Energy Policy, 2018, https://energypolicy.columbia.edu/sites/default/files/pictures/Guide%20to%20Chinese%20Climate%20Policy%207-27-18.pdf> (For the increase in CO_2 emissions in 2018, see <https://climateactiontracker.org/countries/china/>.)

Kohei Saito, *Karl Marx's Ecosocialism: Capital, Nature and the Unfinished Critique of Political Economy* (New York: Monthly Review Press, 2017).

Naomi Klein, *This Changes Everything: Capitalism vs. The Climate* (London: Allen Lane, 2014).

Sheila Rowbotham, Lynne Segal, and Hilary Wainwright, *Beyond the Fragments* (London: Merlin Press, 1979). (Rowbotham on 'creativity in diversity' is p. 149.)

Sheila Rowbotham, *Beyond the Fragments* (London: Merlin Press, 3rd edition, 2013), pp. 24–5.

Chapter 4: Beyond the dominant orthodoxies

Julia Lovell, *Maoism: A Global History* (London: Bodley Head, 2019).

Thomas Blanchet, Luas Chancel, and Amory Gethin, 'Forty Years of Inequality in Europe: Evidence from Distributional National Accounts', VOX CEPR Policy Portal, 22 April 2019 <https://voxeu.org/article/forty-years-inequality-europe>.

Ralf Dahrendorf, *Reflections on the Revolution in Europe* (New York: Times Books, 1990).

For the specific impact of austerity on social democratic parties, see James F. Downes and Edward Chan, 'Explaining the Electoral Debacle of Social Democratic Parties in Europe', LSE blog, 2018

<https://blogs.lse.ac.uk/europpblog/2018/06/21/explaining-the-electoral-debacle-of-social-democratic-parties-in-europe/>.

For continuing support for the values of the welfare state, see Frédéric Gonthier, 'More State Intervention, More Equality, Changing Economic Attitudes in the European Union', in Pierre Bréchon and Frédéric Gonthier (eds), *European Values: Trends and Divides over Thirty Years* (Leiden: Brill, 2017).

For the fall in GDP and the rise of Podemos, see Luis Ramiro and Raul Gomez, 'Radical-Left Populism during the Great Recession: *Podemos* and its Competition with the Established Radical Left', *Political Studies*, 65 (1S), 2017.

The statistics on the Greek economy are from Mark Weisbrot, Avid Rosnick, and Stephan Lefebvre, *The Greek Economy: Which Way Forward?* Center for Economic and Policy Research, January 2015, <https://cepr.net/documents/greek-economy-2015-01.pdf>.

The statistic on the Portuguese budget deficit is from Sheri Berman and Maria Snegovaya, 'Populism and the Decline of Social Democracy', *Journal of Democracy* 30 (3) 2019, p. 16.

The statistics on Venezuelan poverty and inequality are from Mark Weisbrot, Rebecca Ray, and Luis Sandoval, 'The Chávez Administration at 10 Years: The Economy and Social Indicators', Center for Economic and Policy Research, 2009. <https://cepr.net/documents/publications/venezuela-2009-02.pdf>.

The statistic on Venezuela's oil dependency is from Mike Gonzales, *Hugo Chávez: Socialist for the Twenty-First Century* (London: Pluto Press, 2014), p. 131.

The statistics on the Venezuelan economy in 2016 are from Christina Skinner, 'The Legacy of Hugo Chávez and a Failing Venezuela', Wharton University Public Policy, Issue Brief, 7 (7), February 2017, <https://publicpolicy.wharton.upenn.edu/live/news/1696-the-legacy-of-hugo-chavez-and-a-failing-venezuela>.

For the participatory nature of the union in Morales's region, see Mike Geddes, 'What Happens when Community Organisers Move into Government?', in Mae Shaw and Marjorie Mayo (eds), *Class, Inequality and Community Development* (Cambridge: Policy Press, 2016).

The statistics on Bolivia's dependency on extraction industries are from Salvador Perez, 'Economic, Social and Political Dimensions of Bolivia under the Morales Administration (2006–2016) and Key Challenges Ahead', SCISER, 2016, <https://sciser.org/2016/12/02/

economic-social-and-political-dimensions-of-bolivia-under-the-morales-administration-2006-2016-and-key-challenges-ahead/>.

The statistics on indigenous poverty are from B. S. Gigler, *Poverty, Inequality and Human Development of Indigenous Peoples in Bolivia* (Washington DC: Georgetown University Center for Latin American Studies, 2009), pp. 7–8. <http://pdba.georgetown.edu/CLAS%20RESEARCH/Working%20Papers/WP17.pdf>.

The information on language and educational policies in indigenous communities is from Cailin Campbell, 'Are Indigenous Peoples Better Off under Evo Morales? Towards Understanding the Effects of Decolonization Policy on Social Inclusion in Bolivia', Undergraduate Honors Thesis, University of San Francisco, 2018, <https://repository.usfca.edu/cgi/viewcontent.cgi?article=1024&context=honors>.

The statistics on the decline in poverty are from 'Health in the Americas', Pan American Health Organization/World Health Organization, 2017, <https://www.paho.org/salud-en-las-americas-2017/?p=3974>.

The statistics on the changes in the social composition of the legislative assembly are from Santiago Anria, 'Delegative Democracy Revisited: More Inclusion, Less Liberalism in Bolivia', *Journal of Democracy*, 27 (3), 2016, pp. 103–4.

The statistics for women and land ownership are from Emily Achtenberg, 'Bolivia: The Unfinished Business of Land Reform', Nacla, 31 March 2013, <https://nacla.org/blog/2013/3/31/bolivia-unfinished-business-land-reform>.

The statistic on the percentage of women in the 2014 parliament is from 'Women in National Parliaments' Inter-Parliamentary Union, 2019, <http://archive.ipu.org/wmn-e/classif.htm>;

The information on the 'Political Agenda from Women' is from International Institute for Democracy and Electoral Assistance, 'Bolivian Elections Result in More Women in Parliament', *Latin America and the Caribbean*, News, 27 October 2014, <https://www.idea.int/news-media/news/bolivian-elections-result-more-women-parliament>; for a highly critical report on the record of MAS on gender, see 'Gender and Politics in Bolivia: Violent Repercussions of the Political "Empowerment of Women"' *Christian Aid*, August 2017, <https://www.christianaid.org.uk/sites/default/files/2017-09/Bolivia-women-politics-violence-case-study-J29334-aug2017.pdf>.

The quotation from the press release of the OAS Electoral Observation
   Mission is in Guillaume Long et al. 'What Happened in Bolivia's
   Vote Count? The Role of the OAS Electoral Observation Mission',
   CEPR, November 2019, <https://cepr.net/images/stories/reports/
   bolivia-elections-2019-11.pdf>.
Statement from President Donald J. Trump Regarding the
   Resignation of Bolivian President Evo Morales, 11 November 2019,
   <https://www.whitehouse.gov/briefings-statements/statement-
   president-donald-j-trump-regarding-resignation-bolivian-
   president-evo-morales/>.

Chapter 5: Socialism today and tomorrow

Thomas Piketty, *Capital in the Twenty-First Century* (Cambridge,
   Mass.: Harvard University Press, 2014).
Facundo Alveredo et al. (eds), *World Inequality Report 2018*
   (Cambridge, Mass.: Harvard University Press/Belknap 2018)
   available on <https://wir2018.wid.world/download.html>. Branko
   Milanovic, *Global Inequality: A New Approach for the Age of
   Globalization* (Cambridge, Mass.: Harvard University Press/
   Belknap, 2016) is another influential work on global inequality.
The statistics on the extremes of global poverty and wealth are from
   'Public Good or Private Wealth?', Oxfam Briefing Paper, 2019
   <https://policy-practice.oxfam.org.uk/publications/public-
   good-or-private-wealth-universal-health-education-and-
   other-public-servi-620599>.
Kate Pickett and Richard G. Wilkinson, *The Spirit Level: Why
   Equality is Better for Everyone* (2nd edition, London:
   Penguin, 2010).
For survey evidence on attitudes towards social protection, see
   Gonthier 2017, cited in Chapter 4.
Zygmunt Bauman, *Socialism, The Active Utopia* (London: Allen and
   Unwin, 1976), p. 53.
Karl Marx, *Critique of the Gotha Programme* (1875) in Lewis Feuer
   (ed.), *Marx and Engels, Basic Writings on Politics and Philosophy*
   (London: Fontana, 1969), p. 160.
Alec Nove, *The Economics of Feasible Socialism* (London:
   Routledge, 1983).
On attitudes to socialism in the USA, see Frank Newport, 'The
   Meaning of "Socialism" to Americans Today', Gallup, 4 October
   2018, <https://news.gallup.com/opinion/polling-matters/243362/

meaning-socialism-americans-today.aspx>, and 'Democrats More
Positive About Socialism Than Capitalism', Gallup, 13 August 2018,
<https://news.gallup.com/poll/240725/democrats-positive-socialism-
capitalism.aspx>.

For cities and austerity, see Jonathan Davies, *Governing in and
Against Austerity: International Lessons from Eight Cities*, 2017,
<https://papers.ssrn.com/sol3/papers.cfm?abstract_id=3023953>.

Ralph Miliband, 'The New Revisionism in Britain', *New Left Review*
1/150, April 1985, p. 26.

Proudhon's denunciation of the state was in *Idée générale de la
révolution au XXXe siècle*, 1851, quoted in Joll 1964 (cited in
Chapter 1), pp. 78–9.

Oscar Wilde, 'The Soul of Man under Socialism', 1891 Marxists
Internet Archive, <https://www.marxists.org/reference/archive/
wilde-oscar/soul-man/>.

Further reading

Chapter 1: Socialist traditions

Barbara Goodwin and Keith Taylor, *The Politics of Utopia: A Study in Theory and Practice* (Oxford: Peter Lang, 2009).

Colin Ward, *Anarchism: A Very Short Introduction* (Oxford: Oxford University Press, 2004).

Karl Marx: Selected Writings, ed.David McLellan (Oxford: Oxford University Press, 2000).

Karl Marx and Frederick Engels, *Communist Manifesto, A Modern Edition, Introduction by Eric Hobsbawm* (London and New York: Verso, 2012).

Gareth Stedman Jones, *Karl Marx, Greatness and Illusion* (London: Penguin, 2017).

Donald Sassoon, *One Hundred Years of Socialism* (London: I.B. Tauris, revised edition, 2010).

James Joll, *The Second International 1889-1914* (London: Routledge Revival, 2013).

Sheila Fitzpatrick, *The Russian Revolution* (Oxford: Oxford University Press, 4th edition, 2017).

Tony Wright, *Socialisms: Old and New* (London: Routledge 1996).

Ralph Miliband, *Marxism and Politics* (London: Merlin Press, 2003).

Chapter 2: Cuban communism and Swedish social democracy

Ben Fowkes, *The Rise and Fall of Communism in Eastern Europe* (London: Palgrave Macmillan, 1995).

Geoff Eley, *Forging Democracy: The History of the Left in Europe, 1850-2000* (New York: Oxford University Press, 2002).

Henry Milner, *Sweden: Social Democracy in Practice* (Oxford: Oxford University Press, 1990).

Jenny Andersson, *Between Growth and Security: Swedish Social Democracy from a Strong Society to a Third Way* (Manchester: Manchester University Press, 2006).

Dimitris Tsarouhas, *Social Democracy in Sweden: The Threat from a Globalised World* (London: I.B. Tauris, 2008).

Susan Eckstein, *Back From the Future: Cuba Under Castro* (London: Routledge, 2nd edition, 2003).

William LeoGrande (ed.), 'Cuba: Looking Toward the Future', *Social Research*, 84 (2) Special Issue, 2017.

Chapter 3: New Lefts—enrichment and fragmentation

Martin Klimke and Joachim Scharloth, *1968 in Europe: A History of Protest and Activism, 1956–1977* (New York: Palgrave Macmillan, 2008).

Richard Vinen, *The Long '68* (London: Penguin Random House, 2018).

Ronald Fraser, *1968: A Student Generation in Revolt* (New York: Pantheon, 1988).

Tariq Ali, *Street-Fighting Years: An Autobiography of the Sixties* (London and New York: Verso, 2018)

Sheila Rowbotham, Lynne Segal, and Hilary Wainwright, *Beyond the Fragments* (London: Merlin Press, 3rd edition, 2013).

Donatella Della Porta (ed.), *The Global Justice Movement: Cross-National and Transnational Perspectives* (Abingdon and Oxford: Routledge, 2007).

Kimberle Crenshaw, 'Demarginalizing the Intersection of Race and Sex: A Black Feminist Critique of Antidiscrimination Doctrine, Feminist Theory and Antiracist Politics', The University of Chicago Legal Forum 1989, 1.

Cinzia Arruzza, Tithi Bhattacharya, and Nancy Fraser, *Feminism for the 99%: A Manifesto* (London and New York: Verso, 2019).

Kohei Saito, *Karl Marx's Ecosocialism: Capital, Nature and the Unfinished Critique of Political Economy* (New York: Monthly Review Press, 2017).

Naomi Klein, *This Changes Everything: Capitalism vs. The Climate* (London: Allen Lane, 2014).

Ann Pettifor, *The Case for the Green New Deal* (London and New York: Verso, 2019).

Tim Jackson, *Prosperity without Growth: Foundations for the Economy of Tomorrow* (Abingdon and Oxford: Routledge, 2nd edition, 2017).

Chapter 4: Beyond the dominant orthodoxies

David R. Marples, *The Collapse of the Soviet Union, 1985–1991* (Abingdon and Oxford: Routledge, 2013).

Christopher Pierson, *Hard Choices: Social Democracy in the 21st Century* (Cambridge: Polity, 2001).

Stephanie L. Mudge, *Leftism Reinvented: Western Parties from Socialism to Neoliberalism* (Cambridge, Mass.: Harvard University Press, 2018).

Mike Gonzales, *The Ebb of the Pink Tide: The Decline of the Left in Latin America* (London: Pluto, 2018).

Roger Burbach, Michael Fox, and Federico Fuentes, *Latin American Turbulent Transitions: The Future of Twenty-First Century Socialism* (New York and London: Zed Books, 2013).

Steve Ellner (ed.), 'Pink-Tide Governments: Pragmatic and Populist Responses to Challenges from the Right', *Latin American Perspectives*, 46 (1) 2019.

Omar G. Encarnación, 'The Rise and Fall of the Latin American Left', *The Nation*, 9 May 2018.

Chapter 5: Socialism today and tomorrow

Kate Pickett and Richard G. Wilkinson, *The Spirit Level: Why Equality is Better for Everyone* (2nd edition, London: Penguin, 2010).

Thomas Piketty, *Capital in the Twenty-First Century* (Cambridge, Mass.: Harvard University Press, 2014).

Jeremy Gilbert, *Twenty-First Century Socialism* (Cambridge: Polity Press, 2019).

Nancy Fraser, 'What should Socialism Mean in the Twenty-First Century?' in Leo Panitch and Greg Albo (eds), *Socialist Register 2020* (London: Merlin, 2019).

G. A. Cohen, *Why Not Socialism?* (Princeton: Princeton University Press, 2009).

Hilary Wainwright, *A New Politics from the Left* (Cambridge: Polity, 2018).

Data Base for Minim—Municipal Observatory, <https://minim-municipalism.org/>.

Index

For the benefit of digital users, indexed terms that span two pages (e.g., 52–53) may, on occasion, appear on only one of those pages.

Socialism

Socialism

COMMUNISM
A Very Short Introduction
Leslie Holmes

The collapse of communism was one of the most defining moments of the twentieth century. At its peak, more than a third of the world's population had lived under communist power. What is communism? Where did the idea come from and what attracted people to it? What is the future for communism? This Very Short Introduction considers these questions and more in the search to explore and understand communism. Explaining the theory behind its ideology, and examining the history and mindset behind its political, economic and social structures, Leslie Holmes examines the highs and lows of communist power and its future in today's world.

Very readable and with its wealth of detail a most valuable reference book.

Gwyn Griffiths, Morning Star

CRITICAL THEORY
A Very Short Introduction
Stephen Eric Bronner

In its essence, Critical Theory is Western Marxist thought with
the emphasis moved from the liberation of the working class to
broader issues of individual agency. Critical Theory emerged
in the 1920s from the work of the Frankfurt School, the circle
of German-Jewish academics who sought to diagnose--and, if
at all possible, cure--the ills of society, particularly fascism
and capitalism. In this book, Stephen Eric Bronner provides
sketches of famous and less famous representatives of the
critical tradition (such as George Lukács and Ernst Bloch,
Theodor Adorno and Walter Benjamin, Herbert Marcuse and
Jurgen Habermas) as well as many of its seminal texts and
empirical investigations.

www.oup.com/vsi

ONLINE CATALOGUE
A Very Short Introduction

Our online catalogue is designed to make it easy to find your ideal Very Short Introduction. View the entire collection by subject area, watch author videos, read sample chapters, and download reading guides.

http://fds.oup.com/www.oup.co.uk/general/vsi/index.html

SOCIAL MEDIA
Very Short Introduction

Join our community

www.oup.com/vsi

- Join us online at the official Very Short Introductions **Facebook** page.
- Access the thoughts and musings of our authors with our online **blog**.
- Sign up for our monthly **e-newsletter** to receive information on all new titles publishing that month.
- Browse the full range of Very Short Introductions online.
- Read **extracts** from the Introductions for free.
- Visit our library of **Reading Guides**. These guides, written by our expert authors will help you to question again, why you think what you think.
- If you are a teacher or lecturer you can order inspection copies quickly and simply via our website.